Praise for *Mama Maggie*

From a region and a country that provides so many stories of conflict, Marty Makary and Ellen Vaughn have brought us an extraordinary story of compassion and hope. In serving the children of Cairo's garbage slums, Mama Maggie walks in the sandals of Mother Teresa, demonstrating how a single, transformed life can transform so many others. In chronicling her life, Makary and Vaughn have provided a vivid picture of how concentrated urban poverty can be confronted and defeated by education, mentoring, love, and the leadership of women. Maggie and her organization, Stephen's Children, show the enormous, life-changing power that is unleashed when mercy, faith, and joy are combined. The world will be a better place if *Mama Maggie* inspires both admiration and emulation.

— Michael Gerson, columnist
for the *Washington Post*

Mama Maggie is the white angel of Cairo's garbage city. Without her love, shining radiance, and tireless practical help, thousands of lives would be hell on earth. No flash in the pan, her life work is truly worthy of a Nobel Prize, and this beautifully written book brings her to the wider attention she deserves.

— Os Guinness, author of
The Global Public Square

MAMA
MAGGIE

MAMA MAGGIE

*The Untold Story of One Woman's
Mission to Love the Forgotten Children
of Egypt's Garbage Slums*

MARTY MAKARY
and ELLEN VAUGHN

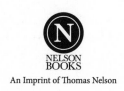

NELSON
BOOKS

An Imprint of Thomas Nelson

Published in Nashville, Tennessee, by Nelson Books, an imprint of Thomas Nelson. Nelson Books and Thomas Nelson are registered trademarks of HarperCollins Christian Publishing, Inc.

Thomas Nelson, Inc., titles may be purchased in bulk for educational, business, fund-raising, or sales promotional use. For information, please email SpecialMarkets@ThomasNelson.com.

Unless otherwise noted, Scriptures are from the Holy Bible, New International Version®, NIV.® Copyright © 1973, 1978, 1984, 2011 by Biblica, Inc.™ Used by permission. All rights reserved worldwide. www.zondervan.com

Scripture quotations marked ESV are from THE ENGLISH STANDARD VERSION. © 2001 by Crossway Bibles, a division of Good News Publishers.

Scripture quotations marked NKJV are from THE NEW KING JAMES VERSION. © 1982 by Thomas Nelson, Inc. Used by permission. All rights reserved.

Photos are courtesy of Maria M. Jacoby

ISBN 978-0-7180-3621-8 (IE)

Library of Congress Control Number: 2014959182

ISBN 978-0-7180-2203-7

Printed in the United States of America

15 16 17 18 19 20 RRD 6 5 4 3 2 1

Contents

CONTENTS

Chapter 1

An Angel in the Dark

IT'S A PLACE THAT FEELS AS THOUGH IT'S BEYOND HOPE. IT has existed on the fringes of Cairo for generations, a maze of crumbling, dark dwellings and narrow streets of packed dirt, trodden by emaciated donkeys pulling wooden carts towering with stacks of rubbish.

This is the place where the garbage pickers live. Fifty thousand of them. They pick up and sort greater Cairo's waste—the trash of 22 million people—and recycle what they can for a few coins a day. They separate rotting food, used diapers, hypodermic needles, broken glass, plastic, metal, and crumpled paper. They live in sewage, disease, and stench. There is little clean water. Among many families, violence, addictions, and abuse are a way of life. Electricity is scarce, and the nights are full of dangers. Almost half the children born here will die before they are five years old. Some starve; some succumb to dysentery. The residents of this place are known in Arabic as the *Zabaleen*: garbage people.

Because of their enterprise, however, the garbage village has its own unlikely infrastructure and hierarchy. Some people have jerry-rigged electricity and established small storefronts and tiny cafés, a bit of civilization in the midst of the chaos. If you visit the area in the morning, donkey carts and rusty pickup trucks are returning from picking up garbage in downtown Cairo, laden with waste. Men are sitting on plastic chairs in the street, sipping tea or thick coffee and smoking *sheesha*, the local flavored tobacco, from tarnished water pipes. Young men are making deals; women walk by carrying large loads on their heads.

A little boy named Anthony[1] came with his family to this garbage slum when he was three years old. He was too young to know that as a Christian in a country where everyone's religion is listed on his or her identity card, he was part of a religious minority. He was too young to understand that his parents had fled from their village in southern Egypt when radical Islamists burned down their home, destroying everything they owned. He didn't know that the teeming garbage village of Mokattam[2] was one of the few places his parents could go to find work. They arrived with nothing.

Anthony grew up in the stench, relentless activity, and remarkable resilience of the garbage village. He and his four siblings lived in a small room under the stairs in a crumbling multilevel building. As a young boy, he helped his parents gather and sort trash. By the time he was ten, he had left school and had a job ironing clothes in an area where people could actually afford such services.

But there was a problem.

The man in charge of the laundry shop took a liking to Anthony. He pressed in on him. If Anthony refused his advances, the man would burn him with the iron. Anthony dreaded the dark evenings, when the man would come after him. He had burns all over his body. He knew of no way out.

But a determined woman heard of Anthony's plight. Dressed in a white T-shirt, plain white skirt, and white scarf, this lady came to him one night, when he was in a fever and a haze, lying miserably on the floor of his shack and resigned to hell. She took him to her own home, far beyond the garbage slum. She brought a doctor to see him. The doctor came every day for a week and dressed his wounds. The lady hand-fed him so he could gradually get stronger—stronger than he had ever been.

The lady talked to him as he lay in bed. She put cool cloths on his forehead. Struck by the stories he told her, she wept. Anthony felt like her tears matched his own. Then she said something astounding. She held his hand tenderly and asked Anthony to forgive her as a substitute for the man who had attacked and abused him. Initially, he didn't know what to think. Then he embraced her.

The lady in white was like an angel, showing him something he had no idea existed. Forgiveness. Dignity. Hope.

Chapter 2

Two Women in the Street

*If you're never able to live for anything bigger than
your pocketbook, your stomach, and your career, then
you'll never be able to bless those around you.*

—Tim Keller

MAGGIE GOBRAN—THE LADY IN WHITE—WAS AN UNLIKELY person to spend her life among the poor. She says that she had no particular skills to help people in need. She had no expertise or training that would equip her to run toward the abused, the oppressed, and the needy. But something happened in her life that turned it upside down and propelled her toward the slums.

Unlike remarkable humanitarian Mother Teresa, who emerged to worldwide recognition from life in a convent, having taken early vows of poverty and chastity, Maggie Gobran came from wealth, privilege, and prominence. She had grown up as a well-to-do Egyptian. Her Coptic Christian family had always paid attention to the needs of those who were less fortunate. She was raised with a strong social conscience. But still, she had maids and vacationed in Europe. She bought clothes in Paris. Her father was a well-respected doctor.

As a young woman Maggie did all things well. She was well educated, married well, had two lovely children, and was affluent, acquiring homes, cars, jewelry, and comforts. She was fun and was admired for her thoughtfulness, her humor and kindness, her many accomplishments. She worked hard, wanting to make a difference for good in whatever she did.

Then, at a time of life when many young professionals keep churning ahead, beating their oars into the cultural current, intent on negotiating more deals, getting more power, and making more money, she paused. Surprising everyone who knew her, and herself most of all, she took a sharp turn away from the next acquisitive step.

A few unexpected observations, along with the altruistic values from her upbringing, began to tug at her. And at a certain point in her midthirties, she decided to make a radical choice.

It began on a day when, with friends from her church and other faith communities, she embarked on what was supposed to be a one-time holiday visit to Cairo's garbage slums. Maggie and her friends came from the suburbs. They were eager to visit an Egypt different from the one where they lived. They were connecting with people who had no social advantages. Many of the adults in the slum could not read; most were barely surviving.

But Maggie found an authentic connection with the children, women, and men in the slum. She hugged everyone, asked for their names, asked about their hopes and dreams.

Intent on mere survival, many had never thought in such terms. But the questions made them reflect a bit, sparking something new inside. They loved Maggie's interest in their ideas, and her confidence that they were creative people. Maggie fell in love with the privilege of being a part of their lives.

She returned again and again, sometimes to give of herself, sometimes just to fill her soul.

On one such visit, Maggie saw movement in a pile of garbage. Digging in the trash, she discovered a baby. Stunned, she pulled him out and set him on her lap. When she returned home, she wept every time she thought about the baby in the garbage and all of the children like him. That baby had a big impact on Maggie.

One winter day Maggie encountered a young woman selling corn in the middle of a narrow, stinking street. She was dressed in rags, shivering. Maggie began to ask her questions about her life. The woman told Maggie that ever since her husband had died, no one had cared for her. Tears poured down her face, and Maggie's too.

Two women, standing in the street. One rich, one poor. They wept together, hugging.

A few minutes later the mother left to go back to her shack to sort garbage. Her young daughter came to take over the mom's job of selling corn. The child's flimsy sandals were worn out, so Maggie took her to get new shoes.

Wide-eyed, the little girl chose a beautiful pair. Then she handed them back to Maggie. "Could I get an adult size instead?" she asked.

"Yes, of course," said Maggie. "But why?"

"My mother has no shoes," the little girl said. "She needs them."

"I went home that day in shock," Maggie says. "I looked at my young daughter. She could have been that little girl. I thought of the woman shivering in the garbage street. I could have been in her place. And I knew something: *We don't choose where or when to be born. We don't choose where or when to die. But we can choose either to help others or turn away. We can choose to do nothing or be a hero. If you want to be a hero, do what God wants you to do. He will let you know what that is, as long as you are open to finding out.*

Mama Maggie's decision to love that little girl seemed small-scale at the time, but little did she know, it was the start of something great.

Chapter 3

Choosing to Care

The truth does not change according to our ability to stomach it.

—Flannery O'Connor

So Maggie Gobran chose to do something for people who had no choice about where they were born.

Maggie would never describe herself as a hero. She saw people in need and felt empathy. She would say that something beyond herself was urging her, in her gut and heart, pulling her to inconvenience and reconfigure her life to help them, rather than choosing to look the other way and do nothing but maybe give some money. For Maggie, it was more a matter of opening herself up to the fulfillment that comes when you totally put aside your own interests and take on the concerns of others.

Maggie wanted to help the poor beyond what she could do on her own. With her husband and others, she figured out a way to do—and multiply—good work in the garbage slums and in other poor areas in villages around Egypt and elsewhere in the Middle East. In 1989, she started an organized effort called Stephen's Children.

Most of Cairo's garbage collectors are Coptic Christians by background, but the organization helps Muslims and Christians alike, as more and more poor Muslims have come to the slums in recent years. Workers and volunteers visit people in their shacks, listen to their stories, find out their concerns, and help them with food, clothing, medical care, job training, and education. The charitable work revolves around building relationships with people in need, building up their dignity, and equipping them to help themselves.

She is now known in Egypt as "Mama Maggie," a name given her by the many children who see her as a second mother to them.

Mama Maggie's work among the poor has garnered the attention of foreign leaders, humanitarian groups, and human rights organizations. Members of the British Parliament, the U.S. Congress, and leaders from around the world have made the pilgrimage to Cairo's slums to see the power of radical love at work. Many of them now refer to her as the "Mother Teresa of Egypt."

Who is Mama Maggie? She is a slender, Egyptian woman now in her midsixties with light brown skin, gray-blonde hair, and an erect posture. She has deep laugh lines; they turn upward, making it look like her eyes are smiling all the time. Despite working in one of the filthiest urban centers in the world, she dresses entirely in white—a long, simple skirt, long-sleeved shirt, shawl, head covering, and socks with well-worn sandals.

But even though she looks like a nun, she is not.

A former marketing executive and university professor, she ventured beyond the borders of her privileged life in Cairo and found something she'd been looking for. Though she now looks ethereal, she responded viscerally to the pain of the people who live in the ghetto, with a core of steel to set things right that had been so wrong.

MAMA MAGGIE'S WORK INVOLVES MANAGING STAFF AS WELL as many volunteers, about two thousand people. More than 20 percent of the workers come from the very slums they now serve. They know what it feels like to live in poverty of body, soul, and spirit, and they know what it means to discover real and lasting change through the love and attention of caring people.

A young woman we'll call Hawwa, for example, grew up in one of Cairo's garbage areas. She met Mama Maggie when she was seven years old. When Hawwa was older, she went to a Stephen's Children's sports camp. Mama Maggie took notice of her.

"What do you want to do when you grow up?" Mama Maggie asked her. "Would you like to be a leader and join me?"

Hawwa knew nothing of the idea of "being a leader." The slum did not teach such concepts. But Mama Maggie helped her understand new things and have new hope for her life. As Hawwa grew up, she pressed toward goals she previously had no idea how to set. She finished high school and was encouraged to continue on in the university. She came back after college to join Maggie in the work of helping other kids in the same way she had been helped.

When Hawwa's mother became ill, Maggie gave her time off to care for her. Hawwa didn't have money for a doctor for her mom. Then one of her colleagues came to see her. She brought an envelope from Mama Maggie. Hawwa opened it. In it was the exact amount of money she needed for the doctor, a specific answer to her specific prayers.

Hawwa is shy when she talks about the values that Mama Maggie has instilled in her. One thing is clear: she believes in many more possibilities than she used to. Before, there were none. "I have a special life now," she says simply. "Mama Maggie has made a huge difference in my future."

It's a common theme among the life stories of her staff.

Mama Maggie has inspired many, many girls and boys the same

way. For this and numerous other reasons, some have been tempted to call Maggie Gobran a modern saint.

She would be the first to say that she is not. She is full of very human, appealing paradoxes. She is confident yet soft-spoken, with nothing to prove, yet she has the instinctive, magnetic charisma inherent in great leaders. She is free in her own skin. She is the first to laugh and cry and confess flaws of every sort.

She is otherworldly, almost floating away in her layers of all-white clothing in contemplation of the mysteries of life and God one moment, firmly in the details of her work the next, giving members of her staff a month's worth of work to do in a concise phone call. (As her husband says, smiling, "You have to remember, before the ministry, she was in business!")

She keeps her friends close, yet removes herself to the solitude of Egypt's desert to meditate and pray. She's disinterested in life's luxuries; but in a restaurant, she will wrestle to pick up the check—and win. She uses words freely, but with great care; few are wasted. She knows the power of silence, and visits it more often than most busy people might feel comfortable.

She laughs in a heartbeat, cheering the small drawing of a cat sketched by a child in the slum. She weeps in a moment, confiding her weaknesses to close friends or thinking of girls and boys she wants to protect from abuse, neglect, and shame. She dispenses small candies to everyone, from poor children to toll collectors and soldiers.

She is the first to notice people who are grieving, struggling, or ill. Once a small child vomited in one of her classrooms. Other staff stood around awkwardly for a moment. Mama Maggie jumped up, got a cloth, and knelt on the floor to clean up the mess. She doesn't seem to mind the things that repulse most others.

Sharing is of paramount importance to her. After staff meetings in her Stephen's Children office—a converted apartment in a Cairo suburb—she passes out bananas for everyone. She insists she is not comfortable until everyone has taken a bite from hers.

In any account of her work, Mama Maggie is careful to direct the focus toward the children she serves and the team with whom she works. She has cultivated a movement of young people who are working in a selfless way among the poor, making a lifelong difference in children's lives. She is confident that they will continue the work they have begun long after she is gone.

Mama Maggie is an enigma even to those most often around her. She doesn't always make herself available. She is preoccupied with the children, or her spiritual mentors, or the history of those who have gone before her in the path of self-sacrifice. She is not particularly reflective about her motivations to sell all she had to help the poor or to live in a very unusual, countercultural way.

For her, it's straightforward: she simply experienced the happiness of serving others and knew that there was nothing else she'd rather be doing. She felt like God had told her to spend her life in a different way from the usual choices of busy, successful professionals like the one she had been, so she changed course. She sees nothing particularly remarkable in her decision.

The backdrop of Mama Maggie's story—Egypt's complex political, religious, and cultural setting—however, is replete with drama. The political landscape is volatile, changing frequently, sometimes punctuated by demonstrations and violence on the streets. Yet the context of Mama Maggie's work, the rich, ancient traditions of Christians in the Middle East, has not altered over the past two thousand years.

The Coptic tradition, of which she is a part, traces its origins to the middle of the first century. The history of Egypt's Copts is bathed in conflict and persecution over the centuries—pogroms from the Roman Empire, Egypt's Ottoman invaders, extremist Muslims, and many others. Yet the Copts' absolute reliance on their faith seems resolute, cheerful, and fueled by love and forgiveness.

MAMA MAGGIE'S EFFORTS ARE BY NO MEANS THE ONLY GOOD WORK among the poor in Cairo, other parts of Egypt, and the Middle East at large. There are many, many unsung heroes who run schools for children with disabilities, kindergartens, clinics, mentoring programs, and other creative, wonderful forms of help and hope for the needy. In spite of Egypt's great strength and history as a nation, the needs of its poor are great as well. There is plenty of work for every charitable group.

But Mama Maggie's story, and the work of her staff, is still a story about who we are as human beings. It's a model, a narrative, and an inspiration. It shows forth one of history's favorite archetypes: the power of one human being, against great odds, to choose to invest his or her life to make a difference for good. And like the best of these stories, it shows how one small person—armed with faith, determination, humor, and the vision to see not just what is, but what can be—can inspire multitudes.

Chapter 4

Beginnings

She was a spoiled rich kid. She did not know how to work with the poor. But God was equipping her for a mission.

—Mama Maggie's brother Hebo

MAGGIE GOBRAN WAS BORN IN THE UPPER EGYPTIAN TOWN of Nag Hammadi. (Since the Nile River, the heart of Egypt, flows south to north, areas south of Cairo are called Upper Egypt, and areas to the north are known as Lower Egypt.)

When Maggie was born, Egypt was under British occupation and had been the site of dramatic battles repelling the Axis powers during World War II. Nag Hammadi was a fairly unremarkable place except for the fact that one of the world's noted archeological finds was discovered there in 1945, four years before Maggie's birth. Two peasants digging for fertilizer found an ancient, sealed jar full of leather-bound papyrus codices. Some of the priceless documents were burned by mistake in the days that followed, but what is left is displayed at the Coptic Museum in Cairo as artifacts of the early days of Egypt's ancient Christian community.

Like other rural communities in Upper Egypt, Nag Hammadi has also unfortunately been a place where Christians have been occasionally targeted by terrorists in modern times. In early 2010, extremist Muslim gunmen opened fire on worshippers who were leaving the cathedral after celebrating midnight Christmas services (according to the Coptic calendar). Eight Copts and one Muslim bystander were killed. Eleven others were wounded. Soon after, two Christian women were killed in nearby villages when mobs set their houses on fire. Coptic businesses were also looted and destroyed.

Christian affiliation can be a costly choice in the Middle East. A Christian in Egypt today does not normally feel threatened as he or she walks the streets; but still, persecution has been an issue that exists and has been a problem in some rural areas.

Recently, religious-based terrorism has escalated to appalling levels in the Middle East, the Near East, and Africa. Today, Christians are killed and driven from Syria and Iraq, abducted and forced to convert in Nigeria, sentenced to death for conversion in places like Sudan and elsewhere, burned and massacred in parts of India where militant Hindus disparage diversity, and marked for execution in parts of Africa and North Korea and other pockets of extreme intolerance around the world. This is also the case for many other minority religions, tribes, and people groups.

In Egypt, one's faith might as well be a tattoo, a permanent and visible marker of allegiance that invites discrimination at best, persecution at worst. There, your religion is affixed on your identity card, which is issued by the government. Some cars in Cairo's ridiculous traffic have a Muslim crescent or a Christian cross emblem dangling from the rearview mirror. Bahá'ís and other much smaller minorities face all kinds of discriminatory problems. People's names reveal their heritage. Religious affiliations are obvious, part of one's designation in the public square, so to speak, and usually immediately known.

Many Coptic Christians are, in fact, tattooed. When they are young, many choose to get a small cross tattooed on the inside of their wrist or at the base of their thumb as a symbol of their solidarity and commitment to stand with their faith to their death if necessary. The tattoo makes it easy for extremists to identify, target, and, in rare instances, murder Copts in Egypt.

Mama Maggie had a friend who was dragged from his car in a mob and held by terrorists. After seeing his tattoo, they showed him their sharp knives and asked him, point-blank: "Are you a Christian?"

"Yes," he said.

They killed him on the street.

But back in 1949, when Maggie was born, tensions were not high. Copts were a distinct minority in Nag Hammadi, but they were well regarded, as they tended to be the doctors, lawyers, and economic leaders in the community.

Maggie Gobran's father was a well-known doctor in town. Her family was prosperous and respected. She had three brothers, Nabil, Gamal, and Moheb, nicknamed Hebo. The boys went to school with bodyguards, as abduction for ransom—an "ordinary" crime, not religiously based—was a viable threat. Maggie and her older sister, Nadia, as girls, were not considered quite as valuable by potential kid-nappers. In true Egyptian style, their house was always full of family and friends, a happy place of food, conversation, and laughter.

Maggie's childhood environment would set a tone of lifelong hospitality for her. There was a natural, inviting, warm sense of community. Everyone—family, strangers, people who just stopped by—felt welcomed. Meals were long, full of laughter, even if the crockery might not all match or the tables had to be pushed together.

This kind of spontaneous life sharing is in stark contrast to the norms in other cultures where personal space is more revered. A spontaneous drop-by visit can be considered rude, an intrusion on someone's schedule. Dinner engagements can be a formality with invitations that might go out a month ahead of time, and sometimes those evenings can feel more like an *event*, long on the décor and food display and short on real camaraderie.

In Maggie's young world, people mattered, not appearances. Whenever someone entered their home, whether guest or family, the room echoed with cheering. Everyone felt valued. Hospitality wasn't formal; it was inconvenient, messy, without punctuality, and happy.

Maggie was a bright child, clever, confident, and full of enthusiasm. She loved people, and there were many in her life—extended family, friends, and adults—who built her up and encouraged her. Part of her confidence came from teachers at school, who would consistently tell her that she was top of her class. Years later she found out that she wasn't first, after all, but she appreciated the fact that her instructors had made her feel that way. She was inspired by the affirmation that they believed in her, and would carry it forward in her interactions with poor children in the future to come.

As a young girl, Maggie would make her way home from school in the hot, dusty afternoons. The bodyguards would be nearby in a jeep for her brothers, and crowds of people would be around her home. There were three front entrances, accessible by steep stairs. There was always a long line of people sitting on the stairs. These were families waiting to see Maggie's father, who offered medical services for free to the poor at his clinic inside the first door. A second door led to Maggie's family home. And the third led to the home of her aunt Teda. Maggie says she could access any of these doors and be safe, but she always chose to go to her aunt's home.

Aunt Matilda, or Teda, was a dark-haired, strong-featured woman who had sensed a nudge from God early in her life. It put her on a mission to serve the poor. She came from a wealthy family, but she found more joy in giving than receiving. She decided that she didn't want to pursue the usual routes available for people in her situation of wealth and opportunity. She wanted to dedicate her life to do something different. She told her parents she did not want to marry . . . and, incredibly, they agreed. This was culturally unheard of for parents in Upper Egypt in the early part of the twentieth century, where marriage and children were regarded as a woman's highest calling.

But Teda's mother—Maggie's grandmother, Alexandra—was also an unusual woman. She had a strong spiritual focus. She used to sit on her upstairs balcony, late at night, wrapped in a blanket, praying, looking at the bright moon and diamond stars in the night sky when her son—Maggie's father—was out. Long before he ever even stepped back into the neighborhood, Alexandra would send a servant downstairs.

"Open the doors," she would say. "My son is coming."

When Maggie was little, her father's medical patients would make their way to Teda's place after their medical visit. Teda welcomed them into her home with big smiles and warm hugs. Maggie would watch and interact as they received food, comfort, and a listening ear. They would tell Teda their medical troubles and sometimes their social troubles as well. They knew she cared.

For many of that day, "caring for the poor" meant simply giving them a meal or some money. Maggie saw how her aunt saw the poor not as a distant group or unfortunate social responsibility but as distinct individuals, each with needs, insights, dreams, and dignity. The poor were real people. They were her friends. Teda was a woman of few words but great sacrifice. Her model would impact young Maggie and plant the seeds that would later define the second half of her life.

"Everything she touched was touched by God," Maggie says today. Her aunt would sit at night, reading and rereading passages from her Bible. Maggie would sit quietly and listen to her aunt praying, pouring out her soul to God, lifting up the needs of others, and clearly enjoying her life of putting others first. How could such a thing be? Maggie wondered. A human being, her soul flying, somehow liberated from concern, in touch with God and full of joy? Maggie felt like her aunt reflected divine Light . . . she had love, peace, and clarity that were from another world. But at the same time she was firmly rooted in this one.

Maggie's older brother Hebo remembers when he was young, perhaps four or five, being "naughty" one day and eating an unwashed piece of fruit from a vendor's cart. By evening, he was ruined with fever. It was cholera, which killed without mercy, particularly the young and the old. His aunt Teda gathered him up on her knees and held him, rocking, soothing him, and praying, all night long. The next morning his fever had broken.

"My aunt would pray with tears every day, for our family, her friends, the poor . . . We would come in and join the prayer, the Bibles were there, everyone was praying," says Maggie. "If you needed something to eat you would go and eat and come back, and people were still praying and sharing and laughing. It was so loving, so peaceful, so pure. Like heaven."

For Christians and Muslims in the Middle East, daily social interactions are very different from those outside the middle east. God is a part of every courteous conversation.

"We'll pick you up at seven thirty, God willing." "God bless your family." "God have mercy on us." These common expressions are embedded in everyday language. For Maggie's family, like most others, God was never far from people's thoughts, and they referred to him frequently. Their faith was elemental and essential, the same way that breathing is essential.

As a girl, something was tugging at Maggie. Maybe she wanted to be like her aunt. Her mother, Fifi, the irrepressible family matriarch, says Maggie wanted to serve the needy and become a nun, but her father said no.

"Get married," he told his headstrong daughter. "Have children. Then you can help the poor."

So Maggie honored her dad. And being the fun person she was, and is, she enjoyed her life of privilege. As a young woman, she wore the latest fashions from Europe, borrowed her older sister's clothes, put on makeup and beautiful jewelry. Her friends called her "the coquette." She thought of herself as "elegant." Her brothers, teasing, called her something else: "spoiled."

Today they all agree that the last thing they expected, the most unlikely thing in the world, was for Maggie to follow in her aunt's footsteps and expend her life for people who live in garbage.

Chapter 5

Garbage People?

*Never doubt that a small group of thoughtful, committed citizens
can change the world; indeed, it's the only thing that ever has.*

—Margaret Mead

Today half of the 7 billion people on the planet live in cities. Approximately one-quarter of these are urban dwellers; some 860 million are desperately poor.[1] They survive in slums in the city centers of Africa, India, Asia, and Latin America, as well as pockets in Europe and North America.

The largest of Cairo's six garbage slums sprouted decades ago. The people who migrated there in the beginning were, for the most part, village farmers who had been subject to economic hardship and persecution from religious majorities in the countryside. They made their way to Cairo, but they couldn't afford to live in town. They ended up in shanties far outside the city limits. Most of them were Coptic Christians, but they knew little of their ancient faith.

Most could not read or write. Most had never heard of God or Jesus. Their religion was not a life decision but simply a designation, something they were born with, like having black hair or being Egyptian. Many who bore the traditional Coptic tattoo of solidarity did not know what the cross really signified.

Even though their faith was more a designation than a personal commitment, they did still know the reality of persecution. In some parts of the countryside, it could be perilous to be part of the Coptic minority. Majority farmers might burn your house, or kill your donkey, or threaten your children. A neighbor who had farmed next to your plot for generations might suddenly come one day, armed, to take your land.

In fact, the problem of illegal land seizure, or "property grabbing," is not unique to Egypt. In many places around the world, poor property owners are vulnerable to neighbors or even powerful relatives who steal their property. Orphaned and widowed property owners are at greatest risk. A defenseless farmer is suddenly found murdered, and the neighboring farmer assumes the land, often without any ensuing criminal investigation.[2]

Given these dangers and economic concerns, many poor Egyptians had no other choice but to flee to Cairo, often with only the clothes they wore, often without birth certificates or identity papers, which meant they could not get jobs. They would make their way to the cheapest place to live: Mokattam Hill, the rocky outcropping overlooking the city that was originally far from the city center, but became closer as the decades passed and the city sprawled. Today it is known as Manshiyat Naser, or the Garbage Village. There are other garbage areas in Cairo as well.

In spite of being forced into their situation, the migrants made the best of it. Individual families and groups of families found creative ways to make agreements with some Cairo neighborhoods to offer their trash removal services. Eventually a system developed, with various families servicing different parts of the city. Hotels and wealthy districts of Cairo were their favorite clients; their trash was full of promise. Other neighborhoods were less desirable. But most in the sprawling slum ended up with some piece of the garbage business.

Today Cairo's garbage collectors have been recognized by many international environmental experts as having created one of the most efficient recycling systems in the world. If you walk the slum, it feels like chaos . . . in piles. The towers of garbage are in fact meticulously sorted. Large mounds of plastic represent weeks of sifting and sorting—a blue pile, a red one, a yellow one, and so on. The piles of plastic are melted, the resulting smoky residue turning people's faces black, and the mounds can then become something new.

The Zabaleen recycle 85 percent of the waste they collect, compared to an average of 20 to 25 percent[3] in the West, where garbage collection is far more expensive.

This is not a dump. The garbage is brought in by the collectors. It is their work. Their dignity, if you will. Garbage is the means of their income, and sorting it is the stuff of their lives.

A typical home is that of the Riad family clan. They have a narrow warren of four eight-by-ten foot rooms. A family of eight lives in the first room, a relative's family of the same size in the second, ditto the third. The fourth room is for the donkey, whose dejected life consists of pulling a cart each day laden with tons of garbage. He is fed before the children. A fetid, overflowing privy serves all the humans. The rooms are full of garbage. There is no distinction between living space and work space. As the trash is sorted, recycled, and sold again, it can mean a few Egyptian pounds per week, perhaps.

In homes like this there is no privacy; couples have sex surrounded on all sides. The stronger sometimes prey on the weaker. For some children, the norm is to expect sexual relations with whatever older person you are sleeping near. Babies are conceived and born in the trash. Many don't live long. Rats carry disease; blood, urine, and excrement are everywhere. Water is hard to find; clean, bottled water is a little-known luxury.

At its best, the slum is an area of resilience, innovation, and hard work. At its worst, it can be a place of vice, despair, and exhaustion.

It is both: a hellish place that is somehow full of hope.

That is why Mama Maggie—and many others like her who are compelled by love—have invested their time, creativity, and compassion into Mokattam and its sister slums, as well as poor communities all over the region.

Chapter 6

The Land Beyond Time

Egypt is not a country we live in but a country that lives within us.

—Pope Shenouda III

To understand Mama Maggie and her decision to "do what God was calling her to do," as she says, one must consider her culture, the air she breathes, and the history of her land, for Egypt is a place where time itself seems to be measured differently from that of other cultures and countries.

For example, Christians there take pride in the fact that their country sheltered baby Jesus, Mary, and Joseph in the first century. They say that the child Jesus took his very first steps in Egypt, and so sanctified its land for all. They speak of the Holy Family's visit as if it happened last week.

As Samuel Tadros of the Hudson Institute put it, "Copts view themselves as bearers of this tradition, both the inheritors of the greatness of the pharaohs and the heroes of Christianity. If some historical events are deemed still relevant in the Middle East, for Copts this is not ancient history, it is who they are."[1]

If you've flown into Cairo, you know the sight of endless, ancient sands, the fertile delta of the Nile River, like a green artery of life in the desert, and the pyramids, rising impossibly out of the earth, as majestic and mysterious as they have been for millennia. The sky above them is the bright blue of eternity.

On the ground, palm trees rustle in the wind. Something about the way the shafts of sunlight hit the warm stone makes it easy to feel dimensions that one normally cannot sense. To stare up at the pyramids is to feel small, to say the least.

The Great Sphinx, another mystery, guards their entry, paying homage to the rule of the pharaohs who reigned for thousands of years of complex and sophisticated dynasties long before the birth of Christ. Their archetypes reflect precursors of Christianity: the belief in an afterlife and their cross-shaped ankh symbol ☥. The ankh was considered the key to eternal life. Each Pharaoh was buried with an ankh in his hand, so as to unlock the gates of paradise.

Abraham, considered the patriarch of the three main world religions, Christianity, Judaism, and Islam, lived in Egypt. Moses, the Jews' great lawgiver, was born in Egypt a thousand years after the Sphinx was built. As a Hebrew during a time when his people were considered a nuisance in Egypt except for their value as slaves, he was marked for death as an infant, hidden in the Nile River, then rescued and raised by the pharaoh's daughter in the royal palace. He was a son of privilege who grew up to bring both plagues and miracles to his adopted land.

Eventually other players came to Egypt's stage. Alexander the Great was born in Greece, was tutored by Aristotle, and created one of the largest empires of the ancient world. He conquered Egypt and was crowned its pharaoh in 330 BC; the great port city of Alexandria still bears his name.

A few hundred years later, Cleopatra, an intriguing ancient yet modern woman and the last pharaoh of Egypt, saw a new world dawning. She did all she could to retain power, aligning herself with Julius Caesar and the supremacy of Rome and, after Caesar's assassination, engaged in a passionate liaison with Mark Antony. Their military defeat, and subsequent suicides, ended an era.

Three decades later, less distinguished visitors entered Egypt. They were a poor couple fleeing Jerusalem, where Rome had installed a megalomaniac misnamed "Herod the Great." Herod had been alarmed by exotic visitors, "wise men from the East." These Persian astronomers had made their way, with Oriental pomp and a significant entourage, to Herod's palace. They had seen in the skies a new star, some sort of extraordinary astronomical event. They inferred that its presence must have marked the birth of a remarkable personage, a new king, whom they understood would bring peace and goodwill to a world scarred by violence.

Herod was no great friend of peace or goodwill. He was troubled, and that meant all of Jerusalem was troubled with him. If Herod wasn't happy, nobody was happy.

Herod felt better when he hit upon a solution. He ordered his soldiers to hunt down and kill all the baby boys of Bethlehem, the area where this new "king" had allegedly been born. Infant blood should eliminate the threat to his throne.

At least one baby escaped. A carpenter named Joseph dreamed a bad dream with a warning: "Flee now. Take the child and his mother and go to Egypt." He immediately set out in the night with his wife, Mary, and their newborn son, Jesus. They made their way through the Sinai, across the desert, and to the Nile.[2]

One can only imagine what they might have felt when they eventually arrived at the great river and its fertile valley. Mary and Joseph must have gazed in awe at the majestic pyramids.

Jesus, Mary, and Joseph returned to Israel after Herod's death, and Jesus went on to fulfill his calling. He proclaimed good news to the poor. Crowds followed him and heard his message of forgiveness, hope, healing, and freedom for those who were oppressed.

Such news didn't go over well with the religious authorities of

Jesus' day. It led to Jesus' arrest, torture, and execution. The religious leaders and the local magistrates of the mighty Roman Empire deemed the problem solved.

Three days after the execution and burial of Jesus, however, odd news flashed through Jerusalem: he had risen from the dead. The news spread. Mark, one of Jesus' followers, made his way to Egypt about a dozen years later.

One of Mark's earlier distinctions, not his greatest moment, had been running away naked, in terror, his cloak torn off by pursuing soldiers, on the night when they came to arrest Jesus in the Garden of Gethsemane before Christ's execution.

But Mark had been transformed and galvanized by his experience of seeing Jesus alive again. He devoted the rest of his life to telling Christ's story. He came to Egypt during the reign of the Emperor Nero and was eventually martyred in Alexandria, dragged to his death behind a Roman chariot. Many Egyptians, noting that people don't tend to die for a lie, decided to become followers of Jesus.

Christianity grew rapidly in Egypt.

At the time, all Egyptians were known as "Copts," and that was the name of their language as well, a mix of what looks like hieroglyphs and Greek. The early Coptic church was simply the church made up of Egyptian Jesus-followers. Eventually it would establish its own pope and its own distinct traditions. They saw their origins in the prophecy of the Old Testament writer Isaiah, who wrote eight hundred years before Christ, "In that day there will be an altar to the LORD in the midst of the land of Egypt, and a pillar to the LORD at its border."[3]

Second-century writings show that the early gospels, first written in Greek, were translated into the Coptic language of Egypt. For example, a fragment of the gospel of Saint John in Coptic was found in

Upper Egypt and can be dated to the first half of the second century. In AD 190, the School of Alexandria thrived as one of the world's great centers of not just theological writings but science, mathematics, and the humanities. (Interestingly, some fifteen hundred years before the invention of Braille, the school pioneered wood-carving techniques so blind scholars could study there.) Meanwhile, monasteries were established throughout Egypt's vast desert, creating a contemplative tradition that continues today.

In the fourth century, when Emperor Constantine Christianized the Roman Empire, Christianity became the official religion of Egypt.

In the seventh century, Arab Muslim armies overthrew Egypt's Byzantine rulers and conquered the country, bringing the new worldview of Islam, which became the official state religion.

Egypt gradually became an Arabic-speaking nation. The ancient Coptic language was mostly lost, except for church rites. By the end of the twelfth century, Egypt was mostly Muslim.

Today, Egypt is a pluralistic state made up of 88 to 90 percent Muslims and 10 to 12 percent Christians, with a smattering of Jews, Baha'i, and other belief systems. The Copts make up 95 percent of the Christian population, with Roman Catholic and various Protestant groups filling out the rest.

The journey of Coptic believers in Egypt has been a long one. Their faith is not just a cultural add-on as religion can be in other cultures. It is core to their identity. As one Egyptian put it, "In other places, religion is a part of life. Here, life is a part of religion."

Similarly, attending church is not just about experiencing inspiring rituals. It's about being a part of an ancient community whose journey has been long and sacrificial. Many live their faith with ease. They don't feel any particular threat because of their beliefs.

Other Christians have been hit by drive-by shootings and

burnings of their places of worship. They feel that their faith is not just a nice belief, but a higher allegiance that might just require their ultimate sacrifice. They identify with Jesus. They are also determined to follow his example of helping the poor.

Mama Maggie, like so many others in Egypt and elsewhere around the world, quietly lives out that commitment every day.

Chapter 7

Promotion

*I had enjoyed an affluent lifestyle. I always liked to be
"elegant." But now I know that to be elegant comes from
inside; it is to love. True love is to give and forgive with joy.*

—Maggie Gobran

IN 1987, AFTER A LONG AND PRODUCTIVE LIFE OF SERVING
the poor, Maggie Gobran's beloved Aunt Teda died. Even today,
sixty-something Maggie cries when she talks about her aunt. "When
I would see Teda praying," she says, "I would forget this world. She
showed me that love changes a sinner into a saint, a poor man into a
rich man. Love heals the sick and turns the weak strong."

Maggie says that Teda was her "sunshine," her spiritual mother
who taught her how to pray and read the Bible and serve the poor.

So Teda's death was a turning point for Maggie.

Maggie's life had proceeded quite well since her comfortable
childhood. When she was young, her family moved to Heliopolis,
the upscale suburb of Cairo. Maggie went on to excel in school and
her university studies. Her sister, Nadia, says that she was a free spirit
and "Miss Popular." She enjoyed sports like water ballet and basket-
ball with many friends at the Heliopolis Sporting Club. She went
out all the time, and eventually received multiple marriage proposals.

"I don't want to get married," Maggie told her sister. "I'm having
too much fun."

When Maggie shared this plan with her parents, however, they were having none of it. They encouraged her to go ahead and settle down.

So, in what was called an "extremely fashionable" wedding, Maggie married a well-to-do businessman, Ibrahim Abouseif. He was, and is, an unusually brilliant, kind, and compassionate man. His family owned a large tea business in Cairo. He and Maggie honeymooned in London.

Life was good. Maggie and Ibrahim had a son, Amir, and a daughter, Ann. While her husband ran his prominent family company, Maggie worked as a marketing executive with a firm that served businesses like BMW. She loved her clients and colleagues, and they loved her. "She was also very ambitious," says her brother Hebo. "She made good money."

Maggie drove an expensive car, lived and vacationed quite well, and was known not just for her humor and kindness but also for her fashion flair. Her kind husband showered her with all kinds of earrings, necklaces, bracelets, and diamonds. She wore fur when the weather allowed, fine leather high heels, and sweeping, broad-brimmed hats.

Ann says that when she was a little girl, she was always proud when her mother would visit her school. "Your mommy is so glamorous!" her classmates would say. Maggie would take them all out to eat and ask them all kinds of deep questions about their lives and their dreams. She would also make them laugh. She radiated energy.

Around 1982, Maggie transitioned from marketing into teaching computer science at the prestigious American University in Cairo. Her life was busy, full of meetings and appointments.

Students loved the tough, witty professor who wore some of the most beautiful outfits they'd ever seen. She was dazzling and fun. And she made them think.

"I would ask them, 'What do you dream about? What do you want for your life?'" Maggie says. "The men would say to me, 'Oh, I dream of a good job, a beautiful wife, a beautiful home.' The women would say something similar. They all wanted what is known as the American dream.

"Then I would show them the poverty of that dream. 'In the end of our lives,' I would tell them, 'we will all ask, "What did I really achieve with my life?"'"

As she posed the question, she would ponder it for herself as well.

Her students were all high achievers like Maggie. They had all grown up in a class within a culture where excelling in education and attaining careers as doctors, lawyers, engineers, and executives are the expected goals to reach.

But Maggie would eventually migrate from being with the best and the brightest to people who were not likely to make much of a mark on her country's social or economic standing. She would soon be struck by the realization that her life would be best invested with the people who constitute the opposite extreme of the economic spectrum.

"I had the best students, the smartest in the whole country," Maggie says. But in the wake of Teda's passing, she sensed that "God wanted to promote me. He said, 'Leave the best, the smartest, and go to the poorest of the poor.'"

Having already gone to the slums on occasions like Christmas and Easter, she began to visit the poor places more frequently. She saw the appalling needs there. She had a feeling since childhood that she needed to do something significant for the poor.

When she was about thirty-five years old, she felt it was time to make a change. She could keep going with her nice life. Or she could do something that would require sacrifice on her part, giving up time, income, reputation, and many other things, for the purpose of helping people who did not have help coming from any other source.

Her daughter, Ann, remembers how her mom would come home in tears because of the poverty and pain she saw in the slum. Ann was young, but when she went to the slums with her mother, it gave her a new perspective on the good things in her life that she had taken for granted.

As Maggie wondered about working with the poor full-time, she felt unworthy. *Who am I?* she thought. *I am the last, the least, the most unlikely person.*

But it was inescapable. She knew that she was being called.

Feeling like it was time to make a decision, she went back to the slums for three days in a row. She walked with the children, holding their hands and hugging them tightly. She listened to their life stories, tears in her eyes. She already knew that many would die young of disease, neglect, or violence. There was no one to call for help. No child protection agency or authority that could remedy the problem. She thought about what she could do. *So little*, she thought. But she could do something.

One day during a visit, she felt particularly faint and nauseated because of the stench of garbage and excrement. She went back to her comfortable home in the fashionable suburb, weeping, vomiting, and crying out to God.

"You are a merciful God! Why do you allow children to die like this? Why would a newborn child lose her sight? Why the atrocities of abuse? Why do some people live like me and some people live in the slum?"

The questions pounded in her head. She couldn't sleep. She saw the children's eyes, looking at her. She saw her own children, Amir and Ann, just as beautiful, but safe and happy.

"The Bible was the key for me," she says. "This was the most solid, clear direction I could have."

The turning point came from this passage:

> The Spirit of the Sovereign LORD is on me . . . to proclaim good news to the poor . . . bind up the brokenhearted . . . proclaim freedom for the captives and release from darkness for the prisoners . . . to comfort all who mourn . . . to bestow on them a crown of beauty instead of ashes, the oil of joy instead of mourning . . . [to] renew the ruined cities that have been devastated for generations.[1]

As she read those verses, written in ancient Israel, Maggie felt like they were directed right to her, more than twenty centuries later in modern Egypt.

The realization was not easy.

"I was saying, 'What? What? What?'" Mama Maggie says today. "I was the last one who could go to the poor. I had no training. I didn't know anything about the way they lived, their culture. But it was clear to me: I had grown up in a good family where I was always receiving . . . Now it was my turn to *give*."

She wept some more. She says she went through something like the stages of mourning: denial, anger, bargaining, depression, and finally acceptance. Yes, it was inescapable. Maggie Gobran's mission for the rest of her life was to try to continue her aunt's work of sacrificial love for the poor.

— *Chapter 8* —

Stephen's Children

The soul is healed by being with children.

—Fyodor Dostoevsky

THE MARKETING EXECUTIVE IN MAGGIE KNEW THAT SHE could multiply her efforts and create sustainable help for the poor for long after her life was over if she got a lot more people involved. She knew that if the plight of the children was more widely known, a movement of compassionate people would step up to help. She knew that if she mentored young people in their early twenties, they would help and, in turn, recruit others.

Mama Maggie's husband, Ibrahim, says of his wife, "She is a sweet angel with an iron will and an ability to make miracles." When Maggie's life focus began to change, he supported her work in the slums, listened compassionately to her tearful stories about the children, and cheered her on as she became more involved in their lives, even as her decisions became more and more countercultural. Ibrahim has an easy-going nature and an ability to let the spotlight shine on others, asking people a dozen questions about their lives before fielding any about himself. Without Ibrahim's support, genius, initiatives, and care, there would be no Stephen's Children today. He and Mama Maggie are a team, though not a conventional one.

Meanwhile, Maggie was facing a good amount of resistance. Some family members and close friends told her that her vision was excessive. It was good to help the needy, of course. But as Maggie passed whole days with poor families, helping mothers scrounge meals and assisting children with homework, she was living more in the slum than in her comfortable home. It was just too much, some said. They could not understand how their successful, charming social butterfly had clipped her own wings to live in the garbage.

Maggie understood what they were saying. She wanted to please her family and friends. But she felt a strong, compelling conviction. She would not be deterred.

Maggie started placing "help wanted" advertisements in church bulletins. Ibrahim helped her interview potential workers. In the beginning, they operated out of Maggie and Ibrahim's flat in Cairo. Maggie's brothers and other family members joined in to help. Her brother Hebo, an engineer, helped with zoning issues. Her brother Gamal, a contractor, helped with building construction. Her oldest brother, Nabil, a noted cardiologist, ran clinics for kids, while her sister, Nadia, and all the family donated money to support the effort.

Ever winsome, Maggie assembled teams to visit the main garbage village in Mokattam for a year. Gradually the teams grew, as did the work. They visited homes, started a vocational center to teach people work skills, and took kids out of the slum to sports camps. Soon there were eight full-time employees. Then there were sixteen. From the beginning, they took vows as they started their work with Mama Maggie. They pledged themselves to be honest, to be faithful and sincere with money, to keep accurate reports, and to have strict boundaries with the opposite sex.

At first Maggie paid them out of her own pocket. Then—unsolicited—more family and friends, and friends of friends who heard of her work, began giving generously.

Churches that Maggie and Ibrahim had supported in the past came forward. One priest gave Maggie a backpack full of money. The bag was so weighty Maggie could not carry it herself. Her son, Amir, who was with her, had to carry it for her. It contained several hundred thousand dollars' worth of Egyptian pounds. Cash.

Maggie was used to giving to help the work of the church. She wasn't used to receiving money from the church to help her work among the poor. It felt strange, but wonderful.

Maggie and Ibrahim and their friends decided to name their organization Stephen's Children after the first Christian martyr, Christ's friend Stephen, who had cared for the first-century poor in Palestine.

Two thousand years later, the poor people Maggie served were children like Samira.

Samira had tangled black hair and sad brown eyes. She was nine years old but had not spoken since she was about four, when she saw her father kill her mother in their one-room shack. She was afraid of everyone and everything . . . except Mama Maggie.

A year went by, a year of hugs and love for silent Samira, a year in which the tangled little girl saw that not just Mama Maggie, but all the people of Stephen's Children, truly cared for her and could be trusted to perhaps help untie the hard knots in her life. Gradually she began to speak and when Mama Maggie enrolled her in school, her teacher made a report: "Samira won't stop talking or singing, she's so happy! Uh, could you please tell her to stop talking all the time?"

At the time, the Egyptian government process to receive permission to help the Samiras of the slums was not easy. In the late 1980s and early '90s, as Maggie and her volunteer helpers were getting started, obtaining government permissions, forms, approvals, and any other type of paperwork was a bureaucratic nightmare.

Churches, for example, were prohibited by law from repairing anything—a missing roof tile, a broken window—without the proper government form, a daunting document filled with very small print, consisting of many mind-numbing pages. To be approved, this form had to be signed, not just by some government functionary, but by the president of Egypt. So if a random church in Cairo needed, say, a falling roof repaired, they had to obtain, by some small miracle, the actual signature of the president of the entire nation.

Getting approval for a new NGO—the acronym for Non-Governmental Organizations, as charitable groups are known in Egypt—was similarly tortuous. It could take a year if everything went very well. If things went poorly, there was little recourse besides giving up or moving to another country. Stephen's Children was fortunate in that Maggie, Ibrahim, and others involved with it had great resources and many relationships with powerful people.

For the first meeting to get the new organization off the ground, Ibrahim took his lawyer to the government's ministry of social affairs, which was responsible for charities seeking to help the poor. The official who met with them was smiling and cordial, producing the thick sheaf of papers they would need for the process. Then she asked for their names.

"My name shows that I am a Christian," Ibrahim explains. "When I told her, her face closed down completely. 'I am very busy,' she said. 'And it is time for afternoon prayers. Please leave the room.'"

After getting shut out of the application process, Ibrahim and his enterprising attorney shook every palm tree and tried every avenue to get around their abrupt bureaucratic blockage, but government approval for the NGO was not going to happen then.

In the end, Stephen's Children registered as a foundation. The leaders had to go through state security intelligence examinations;

they would be called when they least expected it to come in for random meetings to answer dozens of questions.

Some of the same barriers exist today for new initiatives Stephen's Children begins. The organization's leaders are required to jump through hoops to gain government approval for every new school that is built, every new kindergarten, camp, and clinic. Such approvals require exhausting, tedious paperwork and frustrating, inexplicable delays, all while children are waiting and suffering. This work has been Ibrahim's specialty. Eventually it would become his full-time livelihood—a job he enjoyed much more than his profitable business, which he eventually sold to spend more time helping Mama Maggie.

In Egypt, as elsewhere, the arduous process of adhering to government regulations requires the patience of a saint, the creativity of a brilliant problem solver, and a keen sense of the humor of the absurd. Along with Mama Maggie, Ibrahim, and so many others, the main problem-solver for Stephen's Children is the remarkable and redoubtable Youssef.

If you visit with Mama Maggie in Cairo, Youssef will usually serve as your guide, information source, and ebullient humorist. He is the most recognizable leader of Stephen's Children besides Mama Maggie. He is indispensable. He began working with Mama Maggie in 1992 after graduating from college with a degree in commerce. He says he will stay with this work for the rest of his life.

"When I met Mama Maggie, I knew about lots of male leaders," he says. "But this was a woman, a powerful leader, a woman of God. I saw into her character as a person. I saw God in her. She is a great role model, and this is a good thing to invest my life in. I see miracles happen every week."

Joe Cope is a businessman from the Washington, DC area. When he visited Cairo in 2007, he was impressed with Youssef's conviction to work with Mama Maggie for the long run.

"No one thinks that way in the U.S.," Joe says. "It wasn't like Youssef had found his dream job, the thing that would take him to the top and make him successful. He made a clear choice to work sacrificially in something that would lift *others* up, not himself. It made me think in a different way."

Youssef grew up in Lower Egypt. He was born a Copt, but there were no churches within thirty miles of his home. He was not tattooed with the Coptic cross. He didn't know much about Christianity. He had not heard of Christmas. He only celebrated Muslim holidays. He was one of five Christians among the three thousand students in his high school.

Then an art teacher from the school started having meetings in his home on Tuesdays and Fridays so kids who were already Christians in name, though clueless, could find out more about their ancient faith. The gatherings were necessarily held in secret. What the teacher talked about made sense to Youssef, and so when he was sixteen, his faith got personal. He wanted to invest his life in a way that would honor God and serve others.

When Youssef started working with Mama Maggie, his family was resistant. They were concerned about his income and possible risks, or worse. The government had a habit of harrying Christians and sometimes blocked them from advancing high in professional positions.

"Why can't you just do this as volunteer work?" his father asked.

But gradually his parents started to see positive changes in Youssef's life that were coming about through his exposure to Mama Maggie's example. He was becoming more compassionate, more patient, more enterprising. They also saw the tangible transformations that Mama Maggie and her team were bringing to the lives of the poor. Today his parents are regular donors to the work, and Youssef's family—his wife, who used to work for Mama Maggie and is now a banker, and his young son and daughter—support him in his hard work.

"It's very hard for the poor people," Youssef says. "They cannot speak for themselves. We advocate for them."

For example, Youssef had been visiting with one particular family, and one morning he saw their little boy, Philobus, on the littered street. "Why are you not in school?" he asked.

The boy looked up at him, frowning. "It's my teacher," he said. "Every day she beats me. I hate school."

It wasn't on his schedule for the day, but Youssef went straight to the school and found the teacher. "Beating students is against the law," he said.

The teacher was unabashed. "Well, he is very lazy," she said defiantly. "He doesn't do his work."

Resisting the desire to say something awful, Youssef let her know he was the boy's advocate, thanked her, and left. There was no one Youssef could call, no authority for him to appeal to. So he started working specifically with little Philobus on his homework. He drilled him in math and quizzed him on his vocabulary words. He cheered him on when he did well. He made sure the boy understood his schoolwork.

Philobus started doing better in school. The teacher calmed down. And the boy knew he had a true friend and mentor looking out for him.

On one of Youssef's early visits to a garbage area, he instinctively responded to a challenge he hadn't anticipated. The trash was piled all around him, and the mother he was visiting was sorting it while

Youssef talked with her little son. As the mom dug through used diapers, plastic bottles, and kitchen waste, she found a good-sized chunk of fresh orange. She plucked it from the trash, wiped the peel on her dirty dress, and handed it to Youssef.

Her generous gesture was the essence of hospitality. That piece of orange would have been a treat for anyone in her family, but she was offering it to her guest.

Youssef knew there was no choice, really. He couldn't deny her welcome. He gulped, smiled, and ate the orange.

Chapter 9

I Can!

It is said that "children are the future." If we build a healthy child, then we are laying the foundation stone of building a healthy community.

—Mama Maggie

THE CHALLENGES MAMA MAGGIE AND HER TEAM MEMBERS like Youssef face are enormous, particularly in the field of education. In its 2013–14 report, the World Economic Forum designated Egypt as one of the poorest performing countries in the world when it comes to the quality of primary education.[1]

It is difficult to paint a comprehensive picture of its schools. There's a wide disparity in this nation between the uber-educated, high-achieving upper class and the levels of schooling and literacy among the poor.

Few would argue the basic fact that for the poor, education can be elusive. According to one recent study, the base illiteracy rate in Egypt is 24 percent in non-poor families and 41 percent in poor families.[2]

There's a gender gap at work as well; women lag behind men when it comes to basic literacy. Many poor families don't send their daughters to school at all, the result being that nearly half of all young women in Egypt are classified as illiterate. This figure is of course weighted by the urban and rural poor.

For many disadvantaged women, whether in mega-city squalor

like Cairo's garbage slums or in poor villages elsewhere in Egypt, education isn't a big goal anyway.

A woman named Nesma, interviewed a few years ago by the United Nations, said this: "Life goes on, and this is my lot. Even if I were to learn how to read, would it make a difference? . . . Reading doesn't make a woman socially acceptable or useful. . . . We women grow up to marry and have children. That is our role in life. Anything else is a luxury."[3]

Mama Maggie observed the same fatalistic mind-set when she began to work in the poor areas of Cairo. Yet she was determined to gently push through, to make small changes in increments, to bring hope.

As a college professor, she viewed education as a top priority. She believed that the key to changing kids' lives began early on. It centered on equipping them with a new way of thinking. It depended on engaging their minds—their fertile, capable, God-given minds—to take on the challenges they faced. Without intervention from caring friends who knew them and walked with them through their hard lives, they would simply default into the choices of previous generations.

Mama Maggie began to figure out how to establish good schooling for children in the slums. At first she was thinking in terms of primary school students. Then she realized she needed to start with children at earlier ages.

Early on in one of her visits to the garbage areas, Mama Maggie spoke with a young child who, like everyone around her, was a Copt. The little girl shared some of her worries. "Do you want to pray?" Mama Maggie asked gently.

"Oh, yes," said the child. She pulled out a ragged piece of carpet from a crevice in her shack and went down on it on all fours, forehead on the rug, in the style of Islamic prayers.

"I send her to the mosque sometimes," the mother explained to Mama Maggie. "They give her cookies there."

Mama Maggie, who has many Muslim friends, respects Muslims and their prayer lives. But the episode made her realize that some Coptic children were growing up in the slum without any awareness of their own historic faith. She realized that her educational work couldn't just start with the primary grades. It should also focus on preschools and kindergartens, so young children could have a strong faith foundation as well as the basic skills to help them thrive and stay in school.

In Egypt, public schools take religion into account in a way that is foreign to people in the United States. Religion is taught in school. If you are part of the Muslim majority, Islam is taught by a Muslim teacher. If you are part of the Christian minority, you're pulled out of class and given a Christian teacher for that subject. This system seems even-handed, though sometimes minority kids don't end up with any religious instruction at all.

Mama Maggie decided to try to create kindergartens—for children who are considered pre-school age in the United States—in which kids would learn a different Bible story each week—fifty-two in a year—and memorize one psalm each month. That way they would have twelve psalms present in their minds, which would help them negotiate the difficult challenges of both class prejudice and religious prejudice that they faced—not from their tolerant Muslim neighbors, but from elements of Egypt's polarizing extremists.

Mama Maggie felt it would help these minority kids if they could hear more about their own heritage, if they could learn the stories of their own ancient faith history in their schooling. Mama Maggie believed that if they could come to know about their own heritage of faith, if they could learn the Lord's Prayer and hear stories of Jesus from the Bible that could give them a personal purpose and life-dream of their own, they would have a strong foundation for the rest of their lives.

So Mama Maggie and her team began the work of establishing Christian kindergartens through the work of Stephen's Children. They decided to use an adapted Montessori school model, which is based on an emphasis on independence, freedom within limits, and respect for a child's psychological, physical, social, and spiritual development so they can discover their own talents and abilities. Montessori schools also incorporate beauty, order, harmony, and cleanliness of environment.

All this was, of course, a pretty radical departure from the daily environments the poor children came from.

Mama Maggie wanted to target children whose parents were illiterate, many of whom were also ignorant. It is one thing not to be able to read. It is another not to know basic facts about what is healthy and what is not. Many parents were raised in a depressed atmosphere of abuse, shame, and dead-end thinking. Consequently, they were unable to pass on anything different or uplifting to their children. They knew nothing of preparing their children to grow and succeed for a life that they themselves had never known.

If parents could not read, if wives were beaten down and seen as second-class citizens, if practices of basic hygiene were unknown, children had little chance of growing and thriving. They had no tools to climb out of the prevalent life cycle of poverty and ignorance.

Mama Maggie and her team wanted to make the schools vigorous places where young children were taught personal hygiene, reading, math, and responsibility. They could learn Arabic and English language skills, Bible stories, and Scripture memorization. They would be taught a passage from the book of Philippians, which tells them, "I can do all things through Christ who strengthens me!"[4] They hoped it would become a lifeline.

Children and their families in Mama Maggie's schools would also have access to free medical clinics. Their mothers could attend a monthly meeting to get news of their children's progress as well as nutrition and hygiene training and friendship. In these settings, they could begin to feel a new way of thinking and living, a bit of empowerment rather than shame and dysfunction.

As anyone who has worked with poor families knows, it is very hard to tackle issues outside school that affect a child's performance in school. But Mama Maggie was determined to get to root issues, to the core of the things that troubled her kids. It was an ambitious way of seeing things.

But then, as Youssef says, "Mama Maggie is a woman of unusual vision who can imagine things that are not."

Early on in her slum work, Mama Maggie visited a home where the mother had told her, "I can't even feed my children; how can I possibly think about sending them to school?"

Ever since, Mama Maggie had dreamed of a future in which poor children could get a great start with a strong foundation, where their creativity and intellect could be encouraged and nourished, where they could learn to dream big dreams, where they could break the cycle of poverty rather than perpetuate the ignorance and failure of the previous generation. Mama Maggie could see it in her mind. So she decided to embark on her vision for creating kindergarten community centers.

She told her brother Hebo, who is as blunt and funny as he is compassionate, that they would one day have one hundred kindergartens.

"You're crazy!" her loving brother promptly responded.

Mama Maggie and Ibrahim began the legal process and read the appropriate statutes to make sure that Egypt's labyrinth of laws would allow her organization to build kindergartens. It would not be easy, but it was legal. She began scoping around the garbage areas and found a piece of land. It was populated by benign chickens and dangerous squatters, but in her mind Mama Maggie envisioned a clean, welcoming kindergarten community center populated by happy, growing children.

After some spirited discussion with his wife, Ibrahim bought the ratty piece of property.

Mama Maggie dreamed that a distinguished, internationally acclaimed Egyptian architect, Mr. Adly Naguib, would build her kindergarten. Her friends, like her brother, thought she was out of her mind. One of the most prominent architects in Egypt would surely not waste his time on such a small, insignificant, underfunded project, they thought. Even her eternally optimistic husband Ibrahim thought it was a long shot.

But Mama Maggie was persistent and managed to get an appointment with Mr. Naguib. She walked into his pristine office nervous. His desk was as meticulous as a surgical instrument tray. Bracing herself for instant rejection, she asked for his help in designing her dream school.

To her surprise, he asked her to take him to see the land. That was wonderful, as far as Mama Maggie was concerned, but the price of the project had not come up yet in the discussion. Mama Maggie now worried how her shoestring budget could afford this world-famous architect.

"How much is your work going to cost?" she asked Mr. Naguib hesitantly.

To her shock and eternal gratitude, he responded, "I will do it for free."

The next day he and Mama Maggie met at the benign-chicken and dangerous-squatter infested property. Mr. Naguib, the renowned architect, arrived in a gleaming Mercedes sedan, accompanied by his staff. Mama Maggie, the former BMW marketing executive, showed up alone in her battered Suzuki.

Just one week later, Mr. Naguib invited Mama Maggie to his immaculate office. He rolled open a fat set of detailed blueprints. "Do you like it?" he asked.

Maggie could barely speak. Before her was the full design of an absolutely gorgeous building. Mr. Naguib had clearly spent a great deal of time custom designing the perfect center that would accomplish all of her goals. She couldn't believe it. It was perfect. (Mr. Naguib would, in fact, personally supervise the construction as the center was being built—an unusual kindness given his stature, and the fact that the project was comparatively small.)

She was overflowing with gratitude.

As Mama Maggie left Mr. Naguib's office to walk back home, she stuffed the precious blueprints into her large purse strapped over her arm. Suddenly a black motorcycle with two young men on board swooped near her. The guy on the back leaned in toward Mama Maggie, grabbing her briefcase strap, trying to steal the bag. Clinging to her treasured dream in the bag, Mama Maggie would not let go. The driver gunned the motorcycle. Mama Maggie held on. She was dragged down the street, her face grinding into the pavement. Blood streamed from her forehead. Her glasses were wrecked. *I'm going to die*, she thought as the seconds seemed to slow and blood streamed from her shredded forehead and cheeks. *If I don't die, I'll have to wear a mask for the rest of my life. But I am not going to let go!*

The man grabbing her bag fell off the motorcycle. The driver kept going. The would-be thief on the pavement jumped up and ran away. Mama Maggie was taken to the hospital. Miraculously, she had no broken bones. She spent a week in bed, recovering.

From this determined beginning, it's no surprise that the proposed building miraculously cleared government approvals, or that the kindergarten center was soon home to hundreds of children, or that dozens of other kindergartens would soon be built.

At the same time, some government approvals were extremely difficult to procure. For example, Maggie wanted to start two particular schools in Upper Egypt. The government official in charge of the all-important document approvals said no. This was because the kindergartens had Christian names.

Youssef, who patiently visits officials three times a week, if necessary, to leap through the hoops of bureaucracy so needy children can have kindergartens, had done all the meticulous paperwork in conjunction with other colleagues. He waited. And waited. Finally, permission was granted.

Youssef spent three years trying to get permission for another school. Officials would approve one aspect of the zoning, as in granting clearance for electricity, but then deny water access.

In instances where the Christian name of the school is a problem, some have counseled Mama Maggie to just change the names of her kindergartens—call them "The Flower" or something not so explicitly Christian. But Mama Maggie, determined as always, prays specifically for the name of each particular school, and does not give in.

Youssef sees the big-picture perspective. He says of bureaucratic hassles like this: "We face this opposition because we are in the business of changing lives."

Today Mama Maggie has inspired many NGOs that are now

operating nearly one thousand educational centers in various locations throughout Egypt and other countries. Ironically, Hebo—who more than once had lovingly called his sister "crazy"—retired from his successful engineering career a few years ago and now enthusiastically oversees some of them.

"Education breaks the cycle of poverty," Mama Maggie says. And when kids graduate from one of her kindergartens, they are typically three years ahead of other children who start primary school in Egypt.

THE NATURAL NEXT STEP—A BIG ONE—WAS TO ESTABLISH primary schools.

This was to be a different model. Primary schools in Egypt are set up for the ages of six to fourteen. Secondary schools teach students who are fifteen to seventeen. Mama Maggie dreamed of schools that could offer the very best education in Egypt, schools that would teach children who were both Muslim and Christian while giving them a foundation of positive thinking, respect for others, and a confidence in God's love for them.

Like government schools—and Catholic and Coptic schools elsewhere in Egypt—Mama Maggie and her team would employ both Muslim and Christian teachers. Muslims would teach the Muslim students more about their own religion. Christians would do the same for those from their tradition.

And then everyone would be given a foundation in how to live together in unity, to love their country, and to respect people who come from different points of view. They would be taught deductive reasoning and how to think independently. They would learn to articulate the ideas and beliefs that form the foundation of one's life, rather than simply parroting rote teachings. Maggie's schools would focus on ideas that were universal moral concepts that relate to everyone, regardless of religion or lack thereof. Like this:

> Whatever is true, whatever is honorable, whatever is just, whatever is pure, whatever is lovely, whatever is commendable, if there is any excellence, if there is anything worthy of praise, think about these things.[5]

This happens to be written in the Christian New Testament, but, like many teachings at Mama Maggie's schools, it embodies great human values that encourage kids of every background or belief system—or none—to focus on that which is excellent, pure, and positive.

Meanwhile, there are kids in the garbage slums and other poor areas who have slightly different educational needs.

Although primary schooling is free and legally compulsory for both genders, authorities can't track down everyone. Some families take their daughters out of school by age thirteen or fourteen so they can marry. Some feel that girls, since they aren't potential breadwinners, aren't worth the trouble or investment of education. Further, many poor girls grow up without birth certificates or identity cards, as if they simply don't exist.

Mama Maggie started literacy classes specifically for girls who had missed their opportunity for schooling. They are taught to read and are also equipped with basic math skills and receive a Certificate of Competency. This enables them to qualify for entrance to the state school system that had formerly excluded them. Some girls who have taken this course have in fact qualified as two grade years ahead of their peers who had been in school.

Mama Maggie and her staff also saw the need for vocational skills training so that the students were enabled to seek vocational jobs. Her vision was to acquire a factory and have the children learn to work there while producing shoes and clothes for other children. They became known as vocational training centers, and they were wildly popular among the kids.

In the slums, her training centers teach girls how to use looms and sew and embroider clothing, pillows, scarves, and other items. Teenaged girls giggle and smile and operate a mechanical loom that has not been seen in the wealthier countries for a hundred years, but is common in poor nations around the world.

The girls produce amazing works of art and warmth on these elderly machines. These are not sold but given to families in need, and the girls now have a marketable skill. In the economy of their culture, they can go out and get a small weaving or sewing job. This will sustain them and take them to the next step of growth and independence.

The same is true of the vocational training for boys. They are taught how to make shoes, a valuable commodity among the poor. Boys and young men learn how to take leather, form it around a heavy wooden mold, shape it, and nail it into place around a sole. Then, with a few deft taps of a hammer, they extract the nestled wooden mold from their creation. They buff and shine their shoes to make them perfect. They are endlessly creative; they also learn how to take old bicycle tires and make them into sturdy sandals.

Most of these shoes, too, are given to the poor. Some of the experimental models go to Stephen's Children workers. The young men from the slum who make them can go out, equipped with their skill, and find work that is the beginning of financial change in their lives. But it never would have started without the changes of hope and confidence in their hearts that came first.

MAMA MAGGIE'S WORK AROUND EGYPT AND THE MIDDLE East operates in many different areas, not all known to one another. Staff workers in the port city of Alexandria, for example, don't necessarily know the Stephen's Children workers who serve in Upper Egypt or Cairo.

On a recent train ride, a group of young men found themselves sitting near one another on the crowded benches. They had never met. But as the train made its way down the tracks, they happened to notice each other's footwear and then figured something out. All their shoes had been made in vocational centers; they had a similar simple, basic look and yet excellence of craftsmanship. One young man raised his eyebrows toward another. "Mama Maggie?" he asked.

The other young man looked back at him with a grin. "Yes."

Chapter 10

3:00 a.m.

*The tree that is beside the running water
is fresher and gives more fruit.*

—Saint Teresa of Avila

MAMA MAGGIE BECOMES MYSTERIOUSLY UNAVAILABLE IN the evenings. This is an unusual habit, as Cairo is a lively city, with people routinely going out to dinner at 11:00 p.m. When friends and family invite Mama Maggie out for dinner, she smiles and thanks them, but it's clear that she has other priorities aside from fun restaurants or street life.

The reason is that for many years, Mama Maggie has woken at three o'clock each morning and made her way to church to meditate and pray. She therefore goes to bed early, in order to rise in the predawn hours.

This prayer time is the still point from which the rest of the day's activities flow, not just for Mama Maggie, but in a spiritual way, for the rest of the Stephen's Children staff as well. One senses an invisible power, an energy that comes from the flare of candles in the quiet hours before dawn. It then breaks out like a healing flame on the ruins of the garbage villages and poor areas.

In the quiet, Maggie prays for the children. She is organically connected to them, vulnerably at their level. They are her delight and her despair. She often weeps as their small faces come into her mind and heart. She lifts them up from the dark, toward the Light.

Perhaps it was during one of these times of prayer when, many years ago, Maggie got the idea to wash the children's feet. This is an ancient practice of hospitality in desert lands. Historically, Jesus Christ served others by washing their feet, bucking convention since that was the job of the lowest servant in a household.

This practice is a hallmark of Mama Maggie and her many staff. It's a humbling courtesy to receive. Maggie had experienced foot washing in the desert monasteries she loves to visit. The monks there practiced such service and hospitality; she wanted to do the same.

Conscientious as always, she wanted to do it "in the right way." She got a plastic tub and a towel, and after prayer, she prepared to wash the children's feet. She gathered a group of little girls, and they lined up and watched curiously as she filled her basin with clean water. Their feet were covered with sores, scabs, and dirt. Many were cut because of the shards of glass in the garbage they live in. (Youssef's wife, Mariam, would always wrap their family trash carefully; if there was a shattered glass, for example, she'd cover it in paper and mark it "broken glass!" Then Youssef told her that most of the garbage sorters cannot read.)

The first little girl came shyly to Mama Maggie. Mama Maggie had her sit down before her, then carefully washed her face, her hands, and then her feet.

"What is your name?" she asked. "Christina," the girl responded.

Like Christ, Mama Maggie thought. She bathed the child's small foot and took it in her lap to dry it with a clean towel. And there, on the top of the little girl's foot, Mama Maggie saw a little birthmark. It looked, unmistakably, like the mark of a nail. To Mama Maggie, it seemed to be a confirmation: it was as if she were washing *Jesus'* feet.

A few years ago Mama Maggie met a little girl named Gigi. She lived in the Mokattam garbage village, and one day she came to a kindergarten center there. The little girl seemed to be full of bright promise. Maggie washed Gigi's feet and kissed them tenderly.

Two weeks after this, Gigi was at her home, in a pile of garbage. Some families are fortunate enough to have both electricity and shredding machines that reduce the huge trash piles once they've been sorted. Gigi was helping as a huge trash pile was being fed into a big shredder. Suddenly her small body was being pulled into the machine, and as she screamed in terror, her brother pulled her from its jaws. Her life was saved, but just barely. The machine ripped her right arm off at the shoulder.

As you can imagine, this tiny, bloody, maimed girl was full of fear. She was scared of everything. So young, bloodied, wounded. She was the first child Mama Maggie had ever met who was scared even of Mama Maggie.

Mama Maggie wept after the terrible accident, her heart beating fast in throbs of pain. She reached out to Gigi, but the small girl with the bloody stump could not accept the waves of love coming from Maggie's heart to try to reach hers.

"I wept all the time," Mama Maggie says. "It was so awful to think of how the enemy of human souls wants to rob, steal, and destroy, and would even cause this poor child to lose part of her body, so she would feel a complete absence of protection and security."

Mama Maggie prayed earnestly for Gigi for a long time. Then she unexpectedly saw Gigi again at a day-long camp. She called Gigi up to the front and put her arms around her. Bystanders saw a tiny girl with fuzzy hair and a stump, now healed. Mama Maggie saw much more. She was beside herself. "It was the best gift I could ever receive to see her listening as I talked, smiling at the rest of the kids and looking up at me," she said.

"I wanted to hug her and kiss her in front of everyone, and say,

'Oh! I have dreamed and thought of you every day! And here you are!' Finally, I felt Gigi could feel my heart. *She could feel the love that conquers fear."*

Prayers at 3:00 a.m.

Healing . . . love . . . and freedom from fear.

Chapter 11

Friends Everywhere

There is nothing on this earth more to be prized than true friendship.

—Thomas Aquinas

As its efforts to serve needy children gained momentum and attention within Egypt, no one from Stephen's Children was soliciting donations. Yet contributions poured in. For the first three years after its founding, Mama Maggie was unknown outside of Egypt. The work was supported by her family, friends, and contacts from churches in Egypt. Then friends in Europe, North America, Australia, Asia, and other places became interested in the work. They wanted to know more about it.

But as she traveled and continued to advocate for the poor children, she became aware of a hindrance she hadn't anticipated.

It was the way she looked.

When she talked with potential supporters about the programs in the slums and the chilling needs of the children there, she was passionate and persuasive. But it was hard for people to envision the poor when before them they saw a slim, stylish woman with impeccable, expensive taste and exquisite jewelry.

Mama Maggie had already toned down her wardrobe, but she still wore lovely accessories she owned from her marketing days. She wasn't really aware of the aura she presented. She visited with a group in England that was interested in the work among the children. Her passion for the garbage collectors' kids won them over, but later they told her, "We all agreed about the work among the poor. But we did wonder, 'How come God is calling someone to do such a thing, and she is wearing all this jewelry?'"

Mama Maggie says, "I realized that when I talked with people about the work in the slum, people couldn't see the children. They could only see me."

Mama Maggie didn't want anything to distract people from the poor children's needs. She decided to simplify.

She talked with her husband, Ibrahim, and made the decision to sell her jewelry.

Her brother Hebo saw what was coming and responded in his usual way: "I told her, 'You're crazy! What are you doing? Your children will grow up and they will need the money.' And her husband, poor guy, gave her diamond earrings when their son was born, and so many other beautiful things."

Mama Maggie's mother, an indomitable force called Fifi who owns the entire building in which Mama Maggie and many others reside, came running to her daughter's apartment.

"Stop!" she shouted. Nicely. "I'll buy it all! Don't do it!"

Undeterred, Mama Maggie went to the jewelry shop and spread the whole lot out in front of the happy jeweler. There were gold necklaces, diamonds, earrings, bracelets: a pile of gleaming, sparkling treasure.

Ibrahim was along for the ride. "What about the emotional things?" he asked mildly, meaning the jewelry that commemorated the birth of a child, an anniversary, or some other sentimental attachment. He wanted to save those for their daughter and eventually for their grandchildren.

Ever practical, Mama Maggie responded that he could buy back those pieces.

So, says Ibrahim, laughing, "I bought the emotional things, and the jeweler bought the rest."

Some wonder how Ibrahim felt about Mama Maggie's divestiture of her own wedding ring. Again, he is a man of unusual grace. "I thought she was doing something very good for the poor," he says simply. "Whatever she asked, I would do."

Once she sold the jewelry, Mama Maggie's plan was to give all the proceeds to help the needy families in the slums. "Jesus talked about the poor more than any other subject," she says. "But everyone wants more, more, more. If I have one house, then I need a house abroad, and a jet, and more cars, more clothes, more of everything.

"But Jesus says, 'Blessed is the one who gives.' This is a secret. A heavenly principle."

She sold her beautiful wardrobe . . . the suits, hats, furs, formal gowns, purses, and European high-heeled shoes. She gave all of the money to the poor.

She threw away her makeup. Laughing with Ann, her daughter, she looked in a mirror, pinching her face and looking at a picture of Mother Teresa. The aged nun in her trademark white sari looked like a benevolent prune.

"Oh," Maggie sighed to her daughter. "If only I had all those beautiful wrinkles!"

Ann told her mother, laughing, "I am so sorry for you, but you're wanting to look old and simple, and you just can't!"

Mama Maggie, the former fashion figure among her peers, started wearing the one color by which she is now known. White, as in a simple skirt, T-shirt, shawl, and little brown sandals. Every day.

She insists that the dramatic transition was not a sacrifice. It felt easy. She felt free, she says. "It is the moment when you die to your self-interest when you discover the beauty and power in you."

Others were not impressed. People criticized her and gossiped behind her back. Friends told Mama Maggie they had heard people saying, "Who does she think she is? A nun?" (These were some of the same people who had criticized Mama Maggie in the past for "driving a fancy car when she was going to see the poor.")

A friend of Mama Maggie's since childhood, a woman named Mary who now helps her with the poor children, says of Mama Maggie's decision: "Something had happened to her. God told her something. I was surprised for a while, but I know when God asks someone to do something, they should do it. She was ready."

Anyone who had known Mama Maggie before, like Mary, knew her as a woman who was always perfectly attired. So her decision to strip herself of fashion and put on clothing so simple she might as well be living in the first century was particularly significant for Mama Maggie. It was an outward sign of a profound transformation that was going on within.

Ann remembers when she was a young teenager and her mother was the "coolest mom around," buzzing Ann's adolescent friends around in her Mercedes, taking them to dinner, wearing fun clothes, making people laugh.

In spite of Mama Maggie's physical transformation, things were not so different. "She's still the coolest mom," says Ann. "So fun. So available. She just *looks* different. She decided to get rid of the things that don't matter, and to choose the one thing that does matter."

Maggie released her worldly objects and changed her appearance, but held those dear to her close. Mark, her nephew, says that Mama

Maggie and Ibrahim have always had a cherished relationship with each other and their children.

"I would see Ann curled up in her mother's arms, Amir the same," he says. "Sometimes, when I was living with them, I'd see Mama Maggie and Ibrahim cuddling together in the afternoons. They are doing God's work, in an extremely sacrificial way, but still have a wonderful level of intimacy on a human level."

When choosing the clothing she would now wear, Mama Maggie checked with her *abouna*, or spiritual father, a Coptic priest named Antonius Amin who had supported her work among the poor from the beginning. He had said it was fine for a layperson in her line of work to wear monastic-type clothing. Beyond being in line with those who had spiritual authority over her, Mama Maggie did not care what other people thought. Even if her simple clothes were unconventional, she knew they were exactly what she was supposed to wear. There was something incredibly liberating about playing for an audience of One.

One week she was working with a group of children in the slum. There was a little girl who was very timid. At the end of the week, she finally confided in Mama Maggie that she was being bullied. The other kids were teasing her because she didn't have more than the one set of clothes she wore every single day.

"They don't like me!" the little girl sobbed.

Maggie was kneeling down next to her, her arm around the girl's thin shoulders.

"Have you seen me every day this week?" she asked.

"Yes," said the girl.

"Have I changed my clothes?" Maggie asked.

"No."

"Do you still like me?"

"Yes!" the little girl responded.

"See!" said Maggie. "If you don't change your clothes, I don't change my clothes!"

The little girl smiled. The issue wasn't about clothes, really, at all.

— *Chapter 12* —

Metamorphosis

The meaning of earthly existence lies not, as we have grown used
to thinking, in prospering but in the development of the soul.

—Aleksandr Solzhenitsyn

Mama Maggie's decision to wear only plain white clothes was not a huge issue to her.

But for many who had known Maggie before, the outer change was indicative of an inner metamorphosis. This was a talented, educated, successful woman. She loved clothes and accessorizing and had mastered many ways of looking accomplished in a world where appearances—particularly one's professional look in the workplace—are the first criterion by which one is judged.

But Maggie was ready to bury her former fashionista self. She didn't want people to see an image at all, but rather a person. A simple person. She didn't want to project strength or dominance or power.

She just wanted to serve the poor, without any distractions.

People noticed. Friends around the world had seen her as a powerful and attractive go-getter with a great organization doing important work; she was driven, charismatic, and dedicated, like most of the leaders of the charitable works they funded. Now Maggie's physical transformation showed a personal sacrifice that evidenced her total commitment to the children.

EVEN AS SHE RELINQUISHED THE USUAL ROUTES TO POWER that she had had access to in her former life, Maggie found herself more connected with it. Early in her work with Stephen's Children she met United States congressman Frank Wolf, who served in Congress for more than thirty years before he retired in early 2015. A human rights advocate, he was impressed by her demeanor and her work in one of the worst neighborhoods in the world.

Mr. Wolf has never been a flamboyant politician or a person who looks for the media spotlight. He doesn't even like to smile that much. He is in some ways a lightning rod because of his focus on human rights violations and issues of religious persecution. He believes that members of Congress have an obligation to speak out for those who can't speak for themselves. During his time in Congress, he traveled to Ethiopia, Sudan, Sierra Leone, the Democratic Republic of the Congo, Rwanda, and other countries in Africa to see firsthand the tremendous suffering of the people at the hands of corrupt governments, war, AIDS, and famine. He led the first congressional delegation to western Sudan to bring attention to the genocide there. He spotlighted human rights abuses and religious persecution in the People's Republic of China, Tibet, Romania, Nagorno-Karabakh, Chechnya, Bosnia, Kosovo, East Timor, and the Middle East.

Mr. Wolf had heard of the work of Mama Maggie in the garbage districts of Cairo and made a point to stop in Cairo when he was in the Middle East. One day he was visiting a garbage area with Mama Maggie when a large feral dog jumped at him, baring its teeth, growling, and barking furiously. Mr. Wolf's aide, though it was probably not in his official job description, swung his heavy camera on its strap to hit the dog. But it kept coming. Mama Maggie came quietly alongside the congressman. The dog slunk away.

Robert Aderholt, a member of Congress who also believes in the importance of bringing relief and justice to terrible places, visited the slums of Cairo, along with his wife, Caroline. They waited in line at the water spigot in Mokattam and watched as Mama Maggie washed the dirty feet of small children. Then she washed theirs.

Through a translator, Robert spoke directly to the children of the slum. It was a simple, humble speech from a man who normally addresses his august and graying colleagues on the floor of the House of Representatives.

"Hello, my name is Robert," the congressman told the little children. "We have gotten to know Mama Maggie over the last few years. Caroline and I are just very much honored to have the chance to meet you this afternoon. We have a ten-year-old girl and a five-year-old boy. They would love to be here today and play with all of you. So next time we come, we'll bring them!"

Once the words were translated for them, the children giggled and clapped.

"I want you to know how special you are to us," Robert continued. "We are going to go back home and tell everyone about all of you and how you are doing. We will pray for you. Please pray for us! We will pray that everything goes well here in Cairo, and that *you* will make a difference for good in your great country."

Mama Maggie's travels to raise awareness for the poor in Cairo occasionally took her to Washington, DC. There she would meet with international leaders and speak about those suffering in Egypt. A friend of the Aderholts, Vicki Tiahrt, wife of former congressman Todd Tiahrt of Kansas, spent a good amount of time with Mama Maggie during one of those visits.

"It was a blessing to walk with her from office to office on Capitol Hill and see the interchange as she talked about Egypt, the children she works with, and then the lives of the members of Congress," says Vicki. "[A member of Congress] was in a mess with political charges filed against him by his opponents; these seemed to have finally cost him his position. Mama Maggie was quiet as she heard him tell a bit about it. Then she pointed to a picture of his family on the wall. A huge family. She said, 'Do we think you could have all these blessings without trials and attacks?'"

This is a far more Coptic perspective on challenges than many on Capitol Hill might usually consider.

"When I was president of the Congressional Club," Vicki continues, "Mama Maggie came and spoke to the spouses. She was amazing. She told us, 'May God open doors for you, and if he closes doors, may he open a window. May he make you small enough to go through his window!'

"People lined up after her talk to have a private word with her. She has a very special gift."

The sandal-wearing lady in the white T-shirt didn't quite fit with business as usual on Capitol Hill. And sometimes her demeanor and way of dressing had unintentional effects.

During one of her visits to Washington, Mama Maggie stayed at the notably hospitable northern Virginia home of March and Mariam Bell. Mama Maggie had meetings each day, and March and Mariam had busy schedules as well, so one morning they had already left the house by the time Mama Maggie was due to be picked up by a friend and taken to Capitol Hill for meetings.

Mama Maggie, attired in her usual white, came down the stairs from her upper bedroom and paused on the landing. As she considered her day, she bowed her head in prayer, conferring with the Almighty about all that lay ahead and asking his blessings on it.

The Bells' housekeeper, an expressive woman from South America named Maria, emerged from a room on the first floor, a feather duster in her hand. She had not known anyone else was in the house. She rounded the corner and looked up at the stairs. There was a figure all in white, veiled, bowed.

"Hello?" Maria called out.

There was no answer.

"Hello?"

Mama Maggie was deep in prayer. Silence.

Maria raced into a back room on the first floor and locked herself in. Panicking, she called her husband on her cell phone. "There is an angel in the house!" she shouted to him in Spanish. "What do I do?"

Maria's husband talked her down. It was unlikely, he said, that some divine apparition had appeared in the Bells' home. "Just go out," he said, "and check again."

Maria nodded. She hung up, unlocked the door, and made her way back to the front stairs. Evidently Mama Maggie's ride to Capitol Hill had arrived by now, but Maria didn't know that. All she knew was the stair landing, formerly occupied by an angelic presence, was now empty.

She called her husband back. "*Auggghhhh!*" she screamed.

Meanwhile, Mama Maggie peacefully made her way to Capitol Hill.

Near the Capitol, Mama Maggie saw clusters of homeless people outside a shelter. The contrast between the marble halls of power, crowded with distinguished lawmakers and trailing aides, and the dirty sidewalks crowded with ragged men and women, ignored by passersby, presented a dilemma in Mama Maggie's heart. She stared out the car window at the scene. The poor on the street: these were her people.

For the next several hours, Mama Maggie appeared distracted.

She repeatedly asked if she could go to be with the poor people she had passed. Most of those around her didn't know what she was referring to. She then asked if she could go to the shelter the next day.

It would not fit her schedule. There were a number of important meetings set up. But Mama Maggie, in her quiet yet steely way, kept asking. The schedule was changed.

That night Mama Maggie got the people with her to take her to a grocery store. She bought bread, meat, cheese, fruit, snacks, and hundreds of ziplock bags. She spent the evening making sandwiches and assembling meals. As family and friends around her saw what she was doing, some of them asked, "Is it legal to hand out food like that?" "Will the homeless shelter staff mind?" "Is it dangerous?" "Could it create problems?"

But from Mama Maggie's experience, those questions didn't make any sense. She had seen people who were in need and she was going to do what she could to care for them. Her hosts and friends started to help, and the next day they all went to the shelter together. Their car pulled up where the homeless had congregated on the sidewalk. Mama Maggie and her friends smiled, asked people's names, looked them in the eyes, hugged them, and distributed the simple meals.

Those who participated in the spontaneous effort were struck by a simple deed done in complete disregard of logistical constraints. As Washingtonians—in a place often hobbled by bureaucracy—they loved Mama Maggie's "right now" mentality.

MAMA MAGGIE CONTINUED TO TRAVEL THE WORLD AND returned to the United States occasionally, but perhaps her most dramatic visit was in 2011. She was invited to speak at a global leadership summit hosted at Willow Creek, a church in a suburb of Chicago. Several thousand people filled its main auditorium. The session was also broadcast by satellite to 430 other sites around the world, to a total audience of 170,000 people seeking to learn about leadership.

The tone was thoughtful, a gathering of postmodern, high-achieving individuals swigging their Starbucks and jotting notes on their electronic devices as they listened to internationally renowned leaders, most attired in Casual Friday jeans and untucked shirts, the power suit of the twenty-first century.

On the second day of the summit, Mama Maggie appeared at the podium, swathed in her white long skirt, long-sleeved shirt, shawl, head covering, and well-worn sandals. She did not stride forward and "take the stage," as persuasive speakers tend to do. There was no opening joke to disarm the crowd. No high-energy possession of the microphone. No PowerPoint or upbeat intro music.

Instead, she looked gently at the people around her, smiled, and bowed her head.

Her audience here was not made up of needy children or illiterate mothers. These were people with every advantage, sophisticated leaders, strategic thinkers who care about social justice, who make it their business to help others.

Mama Maggie's simple speech was delivered in her soft, accented English. She gave insights into her own decision to expend her life helping the poor. She alluded to great mysteries about what God can do in a person's life. She held no power in their society. But it was clear to the audience that she was speaking with great authority.

This recognition escalated in the huge auditorium as she began to share the joys of loving the unloved. With each word, listeners gradually put down their pens and phones. Many found themselves in tears they could not explain.

As Mama Maggie finished talking, she said, "I would like to end my presentation by thanking and blessing you." She then went down to the foot of the podium, touched her head to the carpet, kissed the ground, and lay prostrate.

No one lies on the floor in America.

As Maggie lay quietly, something happened. Audience members slowly began to rise to their feet. Soon everyone was standing quietly, stopping and bathing in the moment. It was the rarest reaction that could occur in the verbal, left-brain, media-driven, over-analysis, sound-bite culture of the West: *Silence.*

Why?

As one attendee put it,

She is very smart. But that is not the answer. She also helps people, but that is not the answer. The answer . . . is the "whatever-it-is" that radiates from a person who decides to walk in humble submission in the ways of God. Mama Maggie did not scold or condemn, and certainly did not force her way. Nonetheless, when she finished speaking, everyone watching her suddenly wanted what she has, and wanted it more than anything else on earth.

But it was not words that began creating a sense of awe among those who heard her. It was *presence.* Something was pouring out of her, through her, and into those who were listening to her.[1]

— *Chapter 13* —

"Interior Fulfillment"

Faith never knows where it is being led, but it
loves and knows the One who is leading.

—Oswald Chambers

A STEPHEN'S CHILDREN STAFF MEMBER NAMED KRISTINA first encountered Mama Maggie long after Mama Maggie had gone through her physical metamorphosis from fashion maven to T-shirt woman. Kristina lived with her husband and two daughters in a large, well-appointed flat in a good part of Cairo. Her husband was a successful international businessman who traveled three weeks abroad every month.

Kristina loved her husband and children dearly, but as they all grew older, she found that she felt oddly empty inside. Something was missing. *Why do I feel this way?* she wondered. *Life is good . . . We have no tragedies, no vices, no drama. We're happy.*

But her hard-working husband was gone a lot, and her daughters were pulling away a little, moving into adolescence and its independence. Kristina felt restless. She poured money into her home, constantly redecorating, painting, and buying more furniture, flowers, and accessories. Her husband would come back from a business trip to discover that she had changed the décor completely while he was gone.

Her home was beautiful and her life was beautiful, but to Kristina it was abundantly clear that interior design just wasn't filling up her interior emptiness.

This realization sent her on a spiritual search. As she looked for something beyond herself, beyond material things, she traveled to places she hadn't encountered before. In 2011, she went to the monastery of Saint Antony, east of Cairo and not too far from the Red Sea. Built in AD 361, the original monastery has expanded over the centuries. Today it is a peaceful, joyful place, a self-sustained village with gardens, a mill, a bakery, and a vineyard. It is ancient, yet surprisingly modern in its therapeutic capacity to calm and welcome those who come from a busy lifestyle, people who want to meditate about life and God. Visitors come from all over the world.

This monastery is also a frequent site of retreat for Mama Maggie.

Kristina had heard about this place of peace. It seemed a good environment in which to reflect on this odd new quest that was developing inside of her. One day, as Kristina visited one of the monastery's chapels, a sanctuary constructed a thousand years ago, she saw a woman dressed in a white T-shirt, sitting silently on the floor. She thought the lady in white was from India. To Kristina, she looked like a person who wanted to be a nun.

Later, after prayers, the woman gave Kristina a fistful of wrapped small candies and smiled at her.

When she returned from the monastery, Kristina continued her search. She wanted to know God more, and to her surprise, she found herself thinking, *I want to serve God.* It wasn't the type of language she usually used. She didn't even know where it had come from. But here she was, going to church regularly now, thinking about purpose and meaning in life, and wanting to "serve God."

One day she went to a Coptic church in Cairo. To her surprise, the lady in white was there. She recognized Kristina, who prepared herself for more candy. Instead, the woman smiled at Kristina and handed her a piece of paper with a phone number on it.

"Would you come and serve God with me?" she asked.

It was the exact phrase—*serve God*—that Kristina had been hearing in her head. She went home and called the number. It was, of course, the Stephen's Children office. Kristina went there and officially met Mama Maggie and the rest of the team. She had thought that maybe the woman in white worked with three or four poor families. Now she realized the magnitude of the endeavor; this woman and her team were serving thousands of needy people.

When Kristina went to the ghetto herself and saw hope in a desperate place, she was hooked. The joy she experienced began to fill the odd emptiness in her lovely life. She knew, *This is what I want to do for the rest of my life.*

Kristina never would have found this opportunity on her own. But now she felt like God had led her on this search. And as she joined the effort among the poor, she also discovered what she could not find in material things.

Kristina says today, "Mama Maggie introduced me to a whole new world. I love being with her. When we go to the garbage area, the children we serve are so happy inside. They have so much hope that God will do things in their home—which happens to be a hovel where there is barely room to stand. We pray, and God is always providing at the last minute."

For a foreign businessman like Joe Cope, mentioned earlier, the work of people like Kristina and Mama Maggie and their fellow staff is convicting. During his visit to Cairo, Joe remembers Youssef telling him, "In my home, we have two beds. The families we serve have no beds. I am so blessed!"

Joe didn't know what to think, visualizing his comfortable life in the United States. Youssef's comment, and the experience of life in the slums, made him see the meaning of the word *need* and the way he uses the word in his daily life differently.

"I felt that these people working with the kids in Cairo had true wealth, which is spiritual," he says. "It's ironic. In my day job, I'm a wealth advisor. But *real* riches are a lot more than what is in your port-folio. Real wealth has to do with giving to others."

Mama Maggie's staff work hard, but they feel deeply privileged. Just about every day they receive messages about violence, fires, accidents, disease, and other emergencies among the poor . . . at all hours. Like angels in the night, they speed to the need and do their best to relieve it, regardless of their personal plans. They don't consider their own schedules to be of paramount importance. They don't fit in the needs of the poor when convenient. They respond as Mama Maggie would, had she the ability to be in many places of need all at once. They bring food to hungry children, take a family to the hospital at their time of crisis, and intervene when violence and abuse threaten people who have no other recourse.

Most of all, they pray. They know that many needs are beyond their ability to meet, and they firmly believe in a God who can do things that human beings cannot.

This perspective among the many staff and volunteers begins with Mama Maggie. Her focus is different from the razor-sharp mar-keting executive and college professor she once was. Now, say those who have seen her change over the years, she sits on the floor rather than standing at the podium. Her voice is quiet. Her effect is humbly spiritual rather than overtly persuasive and powerful.

At the same time, some people feel she is just plain strange; as Kristina says, among other things, her habit of kissing the ground may well seem eccentric. But Mama Maggie learned early on in her spiritual journey not to worry about what other people thought. She is more focused on needs, paying attention to the small things, not just among the children and families she serves, but among the family of workers she leads.

For example, a staff worker had a fight with her husband awhile ago. She told no one about it. Mama Maggie looked at the woman's face in a meeting. She asked a colleague to check on the worker and see what was wrong. No one else had noticed anything.

But the colleague, after gently questioning the woman, found that all was not well at home. There was tension and discord with her husband. Mama Maggie told the worker that she needn't report for work until things were better. She told her to stay at home, and she sent her a small present.

The woman's husband was flummoxed. "What? You're able to stay home from work, and they send you a present?" He couldn't believe it. What was this?

Grace.

The husband and wife reconciled.

Mama Maggie's work is made up of imperfect people. She would say she's the most imperfect among them. But she wants those she works with to experience grace, forgiveness, and encouragement in their own lives. That's how they can pass it on to others.

THE WORK DONE AT STEPHEN'S CHILDREN IS HARD. As Kristina rightly says, "This kind of work is not for everyone."

There are now several thousand people like Kristina, staff and volunteers, faithfully working in approximately one hundred locations in the Middle East. They don't call attention to themselves. They simply connect with poor people and develop relationships with them. They try to help children get the best education they can receive and pass on principles that can equip children, and adults, to deal with life's rough challenges.

One typical worker among this group of unique people is a woman named Maria. She grew up in one of the garbage villages, and her father and brothers were drug addicts. Her father would routinely beat her mother to shake down money her mom had made working in a little shop that sold chicken.

Maria grew up with a stronghold of bitterness around her heart. She hated her father and brothers, and the hatred was destroying her.

As a staff worker visited with Maria, Maria learned more and more about the power of forgiveness as she felt God's love and forgiveness in her own life . . . and gradually, slowly, she began to pray for her father and brothers. She began to think in new ways that somehow unlocked the pain of the past. She says, "Stephen's Children has changed my life, through love and helping me find a deep, personal relationship with Jesus Christ. I became a completely new person. My brothers have become much better people! I would never leave the work of Stephen's Children, because they did not leave me, at the time I was almost lost."

— *Chapter 14* —

The Persistent Mr. Qiddees

Every happening, great and small, is a parable whereby God
speaks to us, and the art of life is to get the message.

—Malcolm Muggeridge

THE VARIOUS GARBAGE VILLAGES IN CAIRO HAVE BEEN IN place for a long time. Though Mama Maggie's work in the oldest of them, Mokattam, has been extraordinary, it was preceded by some fairly unusual events that created more openness to change. There has been a long, and sometimes mysterious, history of spiritual influences on Mokattam Hill.

In the early 1970s, while Maggie Gobran was still a university student, an unlikely person became the first catalyst for change among the Zabaleen. His name was Qiddees Ageeb, and he is one of Mama Maggie's heroes. He passed away in 2013, but during his lifetime he made a huge difference in this world.

As a teenager, Qiddees would leave his miserable home in the slum before it was light, riding on the family donkey cart, a huge basket on his back, to the Shoubra district of Cairo, north of the main railway station. Once there, he would knock on apartment doors, one by one, calling out his trade: "Garbage!"

One of the apartments he solicited for trash was occupied by a young couple, Su'aad and Farahat. The husband, Farahat, worked as a printer at a national newspaper. He and his wife took an interest in the young garbage collector who appeared at their door each day. They were Coptic Christians. Their hearts stirred for Qiddees, who was of the same faith tradition. His clothes reeked with sweat and dirt; he could not read or write. They asked him questions about his life in the slum. These were the first kind questions anyone had ever inquired of Qiddees. For their part, they told Qiddees about their community of faith and how they would go into villages in the countryside to help people in need.

For Qiddees, such compassion was a new way of thinking. He was curious about the faith that was indelibly tattooed on his wrist but absent in his heart and mind. He asked more and more questions about what it really meant to have a relationship with God. He had thought Christianity was mostly just about not being Muslim and about following a bunch of rules.

Eventually Qiddees understood the message of Christ and decided to become a believer. That's when things became more difficult for Farahat and his wife.

Qiddees had the enthusiasm of a new man. "You have to come visit my people!" he would tell Farahat. His people lived in a warren of drugs, drink, violence, and despair. They needed to know a new way of thinking.

But Farahat had absolutely no desire to go to the garbage slum. He was already doing plenty of good things elsewhere. Wasn't that enough? Why wouldn't God leave him alone and calm down this earnest teenager?

Two years went by. Qiddees wouldn't let up. Finally, one Friday morning Farahat felt like now it wasn't just Qiddees but God himself talking to him, saying, *"Go!"*

Farahat told Qiddees that he would come to the slum after work one day. The teenager told him he'd meet him at the Iron Gate bus station. But Farahat was struggling inside. On one hand he wanted to help Qiddees, and he felt like that was what God wanted him to do. On the other hand he just did not want to go to the garbage village. So he boarded a bus going in the opposite direction.

But his planned escape didn't work. Two stops later, he reluctantly but resolutely got off the runaway bus and boarded the right one. And as it pulled into the Iron Gate station, there was Qiddees, still patiently waiting for him.

Qiddees led his friend through the huge cemetery on the eastern edge of Cairo. Known as the "City of the Dead," it had been there since AD 642. It was a four-mile-long grid of mausoleums and tombs—and home to thousands of living people who had nowhere else to go.

Eventually they arrived in the garbage city of Mokattam, at the base of Mokattam Hill. In ancient times the foothills there had been the site of a limestone quarry whose stones were used in the construction of the pyramids. There were rock formations and hidden caves all over the dry mountain.

Though Farahat thought he had been prepared for what he would see and smell in the slum, it was still overwhelming. Crowds of people milled about in the twilight in the midst of towering piles of trash. Farahat was used to being part of a tiny religious minority in Egypt. But now, every single person he was seeing was a Copt. It was against the law in Egypt to talk about the Christian faith with Muslims, but these Christians who knew nothing of their cultural faith were open and able to hear his message.

Farahat started visiting the garbage area regularly. He brought a friend, Fayid, to help him. But he felt like a drop in this ocean of pain and poverty. What difference could he really make?

One day he climbed up Mokattam Hill, above the slum to an area dotted with small caves. He prayed out loud with his friend Fayid, saying something like, "God, there are so many people here, and they are very hard, wild people. What do you want from me?"

He had hardly finished speaking when a sandstorm blew up, a common occurrence in Cairo. Winds buffeted the mountain, swirling and stirring up the vast piles of trash in the slum below. Bits of paper swirled all around Farahat and his buddy Fayid. One came to rest at Farahat's feet.

To his surprise, it was somehow a page from the Bible, from the book of Acts. It was an account of the apostle Paul hitting a season of discouragement. Then, "one night the Lord spoke to Paul in a vision: 'Do not be afraid; keep on speaking, do not be silent. For I am with you, and no one is going to attack and harm you, because *I have many people in this city.*"[1]

Farahat couldn't help but feel this random page in the whirlwind was for him. He looked down the hill at the garbage city below. Could it be that "many people in this city" belonged to God?

Encouraged, Farahat went on to pour his life into the Mokattam slum. He built a church, a corrugated iron hut roofed with reeds. It looked like a stable and smelled worse. Eleven children came to the first meeting there in April of 1974. Farahat's wife started kindergarten classes in 1975.

Soon the congregation of both children and adults was flourishing. Men quit drinking and drugging; they learned that it was right to stop beating their wives and children. Families started to learn how to love one another. There was hope in the ghetto.

Farahat's faith grew bigger. His vision of what could be accomplished in the slum grew bolder. Things were going great for the faith community, but they needed one important thing. They needed a place of congregation, a centerpiece for worship, service, encouragement, teaching, and hospitality. They needed a new church, a giant one, to accommodate the growing masses.

It was inconceivable. Building permits to construct a church were nearly impossible to obtain from the government at that time, particularly for a group like the garbage collectors, the poorest, politically irrelevant minority in the country.

Still, Farahat and his friends kept praying and hoping. They could not have dreamed that their garbage slum would soon be home to one of the largest churches in the Middle East.

It began one dusty day in the late 1970s. As some men were talking near the small cave where Farahat first prayed for the slum, they found a hole, about a meter wide. They kicked at it and peered in. A cave, right in the limestone. They could tell it was large; there seemed to be a big, echoing space below. Men and women in the community started digging it out. They formed a long line and passed boulders hand to hand to hand down the steep hill.

In the end, 140,000 tons of rock were removed from the cavern. It was a natural amphitheater, perfectly angled into the rock so that the morning sunlight flooded the space. It was as if a huge church had existed inside the mountain, just waiting to be discovered—an amphitheater that today can seat about eighteen thousand people.

Improbably, the government deeded the land to the Christians.

Over the next two decades, six churches were established in this cave area. One is a small building full of religious icons, elaborate art depicting narratives from the Bible. When the church was built, most of the people in the village were illiterate. As Rebecca Atallah, a woman who has devoted thirty years to helping people in the garbage village, says, "The paintings were the only stories the people here could read." In the pictures, they saw stories of hope and good news from the Bible.

Rebecca began her work in Mokattam in 1995 with six volunteers helping three mentally disabled children. Today she and her group[2]—twenty-two full-time workers and fifty volunteers—help more than ninety mentally and physically disabled people, twenty of whom are deaf and mute, and two hundred people who live with difficult chronic diseases.

THE LARGEST PART OF THE CAVE COMPLEX IS AN ENORMOUS natural amphitheater with fixed stone chairs, a sophisticated sound and video system, and a lively congregation. An unconventional place of worship, it is one of the few places in Egypt where Christians can gather in large numbers. It has been a spiritual home not only to residents of the slum, as well as Mama Maggie and her family, but to tens of thousands of people in Cairo at large. And it draws thousands of visitors each year from around the world.[3]

So today, tour buses occasionally include the Cave Church as one of Cairo's wonders, along with the Great Pyramid, the Sphinx, and the golden artifacts of King Tutankhamen. It's somewhat ironic that these buses have to wind through the stinking maze of the garbage area before they reach the iron gates of the cave complex. But visitors come from everywhere to marvel at its dramatic, striated rock walls and intricate carvings set high in the stones of the mountain.

A Polish artist named Mario has created stunning frescoes in the rocky caves and natural formations in Mokattam. In one, Jesus stands in welcome and compassion, his arms outstretched. In a banner over his head, in both Arabic and English, are the familiar words: "Come to Me, all you who are weary and burdened, and I will give you rest."

When you stand on Cairo's dry mountain and think about the

myriad churning needs in the lives of the people below—clean water, food, a lifespan beyond five years, sanitation, education, protection from violence, and knowledge that life could ever be different—Jesus' invitation takes on a new immediacy. How can people in such desperation *really* find rest?

The Cave Church area is full of opportunities for respite every day of the week. There are community meetings, youth gatherings, and all kinds of help for those who come. It has been the place of countless baby dedications, including some for Mama Maggie's young nieces and nephews.

The Cave Church's leader is a priest named Father Samaan. Like Mama Maggie, he was a successful businessperson for many years and lived in an affluent suburb of Cairo. But he traveled to the garbage slum and led a small group gathering there. One day someone asked him, "What do you really know about poverty?" The question stuck with him. It was one thing to visit the poor. It was another to live with them.

To the shock of his family, he moved into the garbage village, and he has now been there for many years.

On November 11, 2011, the Cave Church was home to an all-night prayer vigil for the troubled country of Egypt, uncertain in its course and simmering with civil unrest. It was not a political gathering, and no partisan outcome was called for. The people who came simply prayed for peace. People came and went all night; organizers said the event was attended by seventy thousand Christians of various traditions, including Copts, Catholics, Orthodox, and evangelicals. Shuttle buses were provided to get people in and out of the slum. Members of the Zabaleen community provided security, checking for bombs or weapons, just in case.

There were choirs and speakers from different communities; the event was broadcast on live television. Attendees said it was a time of personal consideration and prayer for their nation. Its inspiration was taken from the Old Testament book of Isaiah, in which God says to his people, "I have swept away your offenses like a cloud, your sins like the morning mist. Return to me, for I have redeemed you."[4]

The people first reflected on their own lives, asking God to help them amend areas that were not healthy. They then prayed for Egypt at large. They emphasized their love for their Muslim neighbors and the hope for a healthy, secular Egypt that could protect the religious freedoms of all citizens, regardless of belief.

That night of prayers preceded some extremely hard times in Egypt's history. Mama Maggie has said, and many agree with her, that the difficult changes that have come to Egypt have been hard, like a woman's labor at birth. But they might well signify a new beginning for their nation.

IF YOU VISIT THE CAVE CHURCH, MAYBE YOU'LL MEET A small man wearing a long, dark shift and carrying a well-worn Bible. He greets many visitors to the Cave Church. He has lived in the garbage slum since 1968, when there were just five thousand people in it. He has been through his own hard times. And in 1978, he experienced his own miracle.

"The important thing was not the miracle of finding the big cave," he says today, meaning the natural formations that created the Cave Church and its complex. "The most important thing was that our hearts were changed. In my old life, I was full of alcohol and drugs. There was evil everywhere here. But when we heard about Jesus, he changed our hearts."

If you talk to him, he will tell you there are three words that are basically the same in every language around the world, understood by people everywhere regardless of their culture.

The first is "Amen."

The second is "Hallelujah."

And the third, he grins, is "Coca-Cola."

Then he will smile again, make the sign of the cross over his heart, and head back down the hill to his slum.

A young Maggie, daughter of a prominent physician, was raised in an upper-class family

Maggie and her husband, years before she began to work with the poor

Maggie with her sister Nadia

Maggie worked as a marketing executive with many large companies in Egypt and later taught at the American University in Cairo.

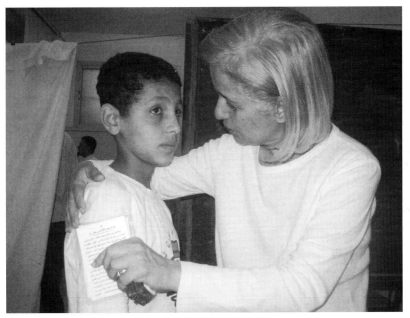

Mama Maggie listening to a young boy from the garbage district

A child at the summer camp program

A class at one of the children's centers

Mama Maggie retreating to St. Anthony's Monestery (built in AD 363 at an Oasis in the Sahara Dessert), where she often travels to pray and seek guidance about her work.

Holding her first grandchild

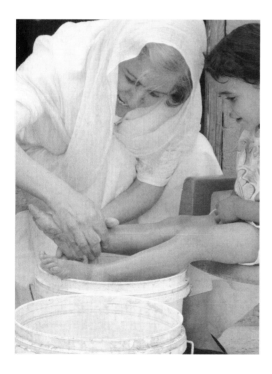

*Mama Maggie washing the feet
of a child attending a children's
center in the garbage district.*

A typical neighborhood in the Zabaleen district

A shoe factory is where children rotate stations to learn vocational skills as a part of their education. The shoes made are donated to the community and are considered valuable, since glass and metal in the garbage district are common sources of injury.

Child at a kindergarden, coloring as a part of an effort to encourage creativity and artistic individuality

The miraculous story of how the Cave Church was created in the garbage district has made it a special place for locals and an attraction for sightseers.

A wild dog sifting through the trash, sometimes competing with the residents there for food

Marty Makary with a group of boys outside of their homes in the garbage district.

— *Chapter 15* —

"The Dead Live Better than We Do"

Wealth and possessions do not make you happy.
Neither does the lack of them make you unhappy.
Our circumstances do not make us who we are.

—Rebecca Atallah, who has worked in the garbage

villages in Cairo for more than thirty years

By no means is Mokattam Hill's garbage village the only place in which Mama Maggie and her friends work. There are so many poor areas in greater Cairo, in other destitute places all over Egypt, and throughout the Middle East where they are endeavoring to spread their help and care. But here's a snapshot of another garbage area near Cairo.

It is called 15th of May City. It's not the tottering, multistory, decaying urban setting of Mokattam, set so improbably against the mountain with its Cave Church and grottos.

This settlement is set next to a cemetery. No tour buses wind through it. It's on top of a stark hill in the working-class Helwan district south of Cairo's center. There are cement tombs painted with bright colors, secure behind a stone wall. They look down on an improbable city of the living, home to twelve hundred families of garbage collectors.

Mama Maggie's workers go there almost every day. Some have to take the crowded Metro, then two city buses crammed with people, and then they walk a mile or two down the long, littered winding road into this community.

This low-rise area has a different feel than the urban decay of Mokattam, though there are commonalities. Children drive donkey carts piled high with garbage, bringing it from Cairo back to their homes for sorting and recycling. Along the path there are heaps of dry stone, litter, dust, and trash. Smoky fires throw more heat and ash into the thick air; wild dogs snap and growl as they chew on the carcass of a dead donkey.

If you visit this area, you'll see low walls of stone, makeshift huts, children squatting in piles of waste and trash. There is a huge pile of garbage that had already been sorted . . . a pile of dresses, shirts, pants, discarded garments that will clothe the families in this place. Halfway up the pile, a large, feral dog is defecating into the clothing.

A broken doll is sprawled facedown in the dust, a picture of children here whose innocence has been discarded. Clouds of flies buzz everywhere.

You step through a low doorway and arrive at Mama Maggie's kindergarten complex.

Two workers—beautiful young women with shining black hair, bright eyes, and huge smiles—sit with a tub of clean, soapy water, washing the head of a small boy who laughs as they rinse him off and towel his dark hair dry. Then they put his filthy feet in the water, tenderly washing each toe, and dry them with more clean towels. A doctor named Abraam stands by to treat the deep cut they find on his foot. Meanwhile, three tiny children, covered with dirt, wait patiently for their turn to be washed.

Next door is a small classroom. Three teachers lead the children there. They greet visitors first in Arabic, and then in English.

When the rains do come to this parched and desolate ravine, the whole area floods. The dead on the crest of the hill, secure in their concrete tombs above, stay dry. The living, below, are defenseless in their valley of garbage. The rains flood their homes; rushing rivers of filthy water carry away what little they do have. As one resident says, pointing up at the brightly painted, dry mausoleums, "See that? The dead live better than we do!"

Next stop is a class for mothers of small children. The class includes education about family planning, women's health issues, how to deal with abuse and deadbeat fathers, and how to raise children well.

It hasn't started yet, but you can see smiling women walking toward classrooms from all over the little community. Next is a class for girls aged eight to fourteen who have missed their chance for schooling. (In Egypt, if you don't enroll in school by a certain age, the window of opportunity closes and you may not enroll.) These girls, however, are getting a second chance and are learning how to read and write. In a place where women are devalued, abused, and often powerless, this kind and personal attention gives them hope, confidence, and opportunity.

The last two stops are home visits, where Stephen's Children workers visit families each week, hearing their stories, learning their needs, praying with them, and bringing food, friendship, and help.

In the first house, a patient young teacher sits on a dirty rug with nine little boys clustered around him. The leader has his Bible open; he's telling a story about Jesus healing a man suffering from paralysis.[1] One boy's hand shoots up. "What's paralysis?" he asks. The teacher explains. The little boys' eyes are intent on their older friend; they don't want to miss anything.

The leader goes on. After all, the most amazing part of this story isn't just the healing of this paralytic, but what preceded it. "Son," Jesus said to the disabled man, "your sins are forgiven."

"How can Jesus forgive sins?" the teacher asks the little boys. They have no idea, really, how to answer this enormous, metaphysical question.

"He can forgive sins because he is God. He can forgive our sins too!"

In the corner, the mother of the home listens intently as well, missing no part of this story of hope and forgiveness. She is due, in twenty days, to deliver her third child, a child who will live in squalor . . . yet her face is full of peace. She has learned, through her friendship with Mama Maggie, that though she is poor in material things, she can be rich in spirit.

In another home is an enclosure where a bunch of big, black pigs—and a litter of enthusiastic adolescent piglets—root about in the garbage.

If you've been in impoverished settings in developing nations, you've probably seen poor people who raise pigs. It's unusual, however, to see humans living in the same conditions as the pigs. Here, the pigs are in a wooden pen, digging through garbage, looking for something to sustain them. The people, in their makeshift enclosures, do the same.

In the main area for the human family, another Stephen's Children worker, who visits weekly, is surrounded by a group of little boys. A neighbor stumbles through the open doorway. He is perhaps thirty years old, one of seventeen children born to the same parents in a nearby hovel. He has the mind of a four-year-old and clutches a toddler's toy pulled from the garbage. It is a toy cell phone that, incredibly, still works.

The man-child pushes the buttons over and over, grinning when his garish toy plays its repeating ringtones. He is covered with dirt, his clothing in tatters. The children ignore his interruptions and finish their prayer. Then it's time for a group photo . . . and the kids pull the man into their little circle of life, so he can be part of the picture too.

Chapter 16

Slow Going

Love seeketh not itself to please,
Nor for itself hath any care,
But for another gives its ease,
And builds a heaven in hell's despair.

—William Blake, from "The Clod and the Pebble"

How do you begin to bring lasting change in a place like the 15th of May slum?

It takes time, patience, and perseverance.

In Egypt, whether one is dealing with the poorest of the poor or richest of the rich, the family unit is central. In the West, there is a tremendous emphasis on individual rights. In Egypt, interest in the community seems to supersede individual interests. People are seldom solitary. If they are going somewhere, they take a friend or family member—or someone they just met on the street—along.

In some wealthier countries, particularly in North America, the culture promotes independence. Many individuals relocate according to schooling and work opportunities alone, even if that means being far from family and friends.

But in Egypt, the mind-set is more communitarian, rather than individualistic. People are energized by one another. Families often end up living together. It's not uncommon to have extended families in the same apartment building, with grown kids downstairs, parents upstairs, and various sisters and brothers, cousins, grandchildren, and other relatives all living in close proximity.

This is how Mama Maggie lived and lives, and it's commonplace for her staff as well. It is also the case in the slums. So for cultural and practical reasons, Mama Maggie's work deals not just with individuals but with family units. So when Youssef and Mama Maggie and others began making plans to set up a new community center in the 15 May area, they knew they had to begin building relationships with the families for it to be successful.

Youssef would come and drive down the long, littered road into the neighborhood, periodically getting out of the battered Isuzu and walking up and down the rows of shanties. Sometimes he would bring a soccer ball; boys would appear out of nowhere to kick it around with him. He'd ask if he could come to their homes. He would meet their mothers and gradually, bit by bit, win their trust. Adults would vouch for him to their neighbors; children loved him. He established connections and slowly and patiently built the foundation for their work.

ONE OF YOUSSEF'S COLLEAGUES, DR. ABRAAM, HAS BEEN helping Mama Maggie for decades care for the families in the slums. As a medical professional, his service has been with the many physical problems the work encounters, from small to large.

"My profession is love," he says.

Often taking a bus to the slums, he works long hours there to serve the people. Through love, applied in bandages, the cleansing of wounds, and the lavish expenditure of time, he brings healing to a place of trauma.

He was once visiting with an elderly lady who had a diabetes-related ulcer. She told Mama Maggie, "You have an angel in your group. He comes every day to change my bandages." She was speaking of Dr. Abraam.

In a congested, littered home with three children and extended family members, the father was smoking *sheesha*. He lit the gas cylinder for his pipe, and it exploded. Everything in the house, which was full of trash, caught on fire. The father, three children, and uncle were covered with terrible burns.

The neighbors—who had next to nothing—took in the homeless family. Mama Maggie's workers cleaned out the structure and began to repair and renovate it. And Dr. Abraam came every single day to help the burned family.

He would start with the seventeen-year-old daughter, changing her dressings, applying antiseptic cream, patiently treating the terrible wounds, then reapplying bandages. Then the uncle. Then he would move to the small children. All three of them had awful burns on their legs. Dr. Abraam applied healing cream to everyone's burns, asking questions and listening to the family's needs all the while. The treatment called for reapplication every four hours . . . and so by the time Dr. Abraam had finished the exhausting regime of wound care for five people, the hours would have elapsed and it was time to start over again. He was relentless.

In the end, after weeks of this kind of care, each person had healed from their wounds—without scars.

Chapter 17

Pigs and Politics

*We think sometimes that poverty is only being hungry,
naked and homeless. The poverty of being unwanted,
unloved and uncared for is the greatest poverty. We must
start in our own homes to remedy this kind of poverty.*

—Mother Teresa

THE PIGS IN THE 15TH OF MAY NEIGHBORHOOD WHERE Youssef and Dr. Abraam and the Stephen's Children "angels" and others work are, in fact, clandestine swine.

Until 2009, pigs were a lifeline for the Zabaleen. Many of the garbage pickers had fled from religious threats in the rural countryside to Cairo. They settled where they could afford to live, together with others like them. To help protect themselves from the kind of extremist religious persecution they had known before, they turned to an organic deterrent: pigs. Since pigs are unclean for Muslims, the members of that faith system would stay away from a neighborhood that cultivated swine. Furthermore, pigs eat trash.

So for years, in the midst of their significant deprivations and all kinds of problems, at least the garbage people and the pigs had a good thing going.

Then, in 2009, the Egyptian government under Hosni Mubarak ordered the slaughter of the country's entire population of pigs, some 300,000 animals. This was deemed a precaution against a potential outbreak of swine flu, though no cases had been reported in Egypt. The H1N1 virus had sickened one thousand people elsewhere around the world and killed twenty-seven. The World Health Organization criticized Egypt's decision to kill its pigs as unnecessary. The WHO said the virus was spread by humans, not pork products.

The government responded that hygienic problems were posed by pigs and garbage dumps in its capital. It announced plans to establish new, hygienic pig farms using imported animals that could be set up within two years.

There was an outcry from the garbage collectors, who obviously do not have the most persuasive lobby in the public square.

Whether sectarian warfare was the Mubarak government's intention or not, it still managed to wreak havoc on the lives of its most vulnerable citizens and create a disaster on the streets of Cairo.

In spite of the killing of the pigs, there were still eight hundred confirmed cases of H1N1 in Egypt and two related deaths.

And in spite of the government's assurances that the Zabaleen would be reimbursed for the pigs they handed over, and that the pigs would be culled humanely, compensation either did not happen or the garbage pickers were given much less than they could have sold their pigs for in the marketplace. And reporters from a Cairo newspaper captured video footage of live piglets being dropped into dump trucks, stabbed, and beaten. The result of the inept mess was that many poor families' source of both revenue and sustenance was kicked out from under them. Deprived and robbed of their pigs, the Zabaleen stopped collecting organic waste since they had no way to dispose of it.

They continued picking up recyclable trash, but mountains of stinking food byproducts, waste, and sewage piled up on Cairo's streets.

THIS WAS NOT THE FIRST TIME THE GOVERNMENT HAD moved against the Zabaleen. In 2004, the Mubarak administration contracted with several European corporations to collect Cairo's trash, cutting off the Coptic garbage pickers from their traditional livelihood. The waste management firms left large bins in the residential streets and charged people for garbage pick-up through their electric bills.

But city dwellers were not used to going down to the street from their high-rise apartments to put their trash in shiny bins. They were used to "their" garbage collector coming to their door to get their trash. So while there was still work for the Zabaleen, Cairo's residents didn't want to pay twice for garbage removal. They cut payments to the Zabaleen, by about 75 percent in some cases. The garbage firms also hired middlemen trash pickers of their own—not the Zabaleen— further crippling the economies of poor slum families that were barely eking out a living.

Community leaders from the slums and others tried to make a case for the Zabaleen to the government but were met with little receptivity. Clandestine trash collection still went on, of course, but the garbage pickers had a rough time of it.

This was the case for ten years. But in 2014, there was some good news for the sidelined Zabaleen. The Egyptian government reversed their decision, accepting that the corporatization of waste disposal in Cairo had been a "resounding failure," and paving "the way for the formal integration of the Zabaleen . . . into the city's official refuse collection system.

"'The others have failed, be they the government or the foreign companies, and now [the Zabaleen] should get a turn, having been sidelined for so long,' said Laila Iskandar, Egypt's environment minister in early 2014. 'They are the people who have the longest experience in refuse collection.'"[1]

A gradual change has occurred in the garbage villages since the government killed off the pigs in 2009. Without the presence of the "unclean" pigs, poor Muslims began moving to the garbage areas, making an inroad into slum communities that had previously been entirely populated by Coptic Christians.

For Mama Maggie and her team this just meant they have more needy people to love and serve.

Chapter 18

The Mama Maggie Cup

*Mama, once I was with you in a camp. I was about to
commit suicide. I had no mother. You came and hugged me,
and told me that "I can do everything in Christ who gives
me strength." Since that camp my whole life was changed.
Jesus gave me a new heart and a new life. Now I am a
successful businessman. I just want you to be happy!*

—a boy from the slum, now grown up, approaching
Mama Maggie in a chance encounter on the street

MAMA MAGGIE FIGURED OUT EARLY ON THAT CAMPS would be central to imparting a new way of thinking to poor children. Once trusting relationships with poor kids had been established and once families would see how their kids matured with Mama Maggie, she won their trust to move things to the next step, taking the children out of their difficult home environments for a few days. Mama Maggie started the bi-annual camps right at the beginning of her work, and they continue to be the place where, as Youssef puts it, "We can harvest what we've been doing all year."

A staff worker, Milad, had trained to be an attorney. He is a tall, precise man with glasses and a thoughtful look. Driven all his life to work among the "best," to his surprise he found himself interviewing with Mama Maggie and joining her work among the "least."

His first time with the kids at a camp changed him forever. He said, "When I saw the love for the children there, I felt I was in another world. I was in heaven. Things at home, things in the field I was trained for, just didn't seem as interesting."

For the first twenty-five years of their work, Mama Maggie rented buildings for their three-day camps. Now she has her own beautiful facility. Buses bring loads of children from the slum. Youssef explains that many of them have never ridden a bus, never gone beyond the commute of garbage runs, never been in a different environment. One boy, reaching the camp and seeing his lodging, yelled out, "Yes, my dream has come true!"

"What?" Youssef asked him.

"To sleep in a bed!"

Another child surprised Youssef in a similar way. As he was welcomed to the camp, a staff member called out his name for check-in. "Kirolos!"

The little boy jumped up and went to the front of the room. "That's the first time in my life that someone called me by my name!" he said.

The children usually spend three days at camp. Staff workers pray for these days to have a positive impact on the community. They know the camps are about more than soccer, play, and fun.

They bring the children into a central area. They cut their fingernails, clean their ears, and delouse them if necessary. They clean the kids' exteriors so they can begin to feel clean inside. Then they divide them into small groups by gender.

But this is not camp in terms of how wealthy kids think of camp in other countries.

At 6:00 a.m., the children are wakened. They wash, dress, and eat a simple breakfast. They sing, memorize cheers and verses from the Bible, and listen to inspirational talks. They meet in small groups with leaders to discuss their struggles.

They have a hot lunch, which is unheard of in their regular lives. One child told a volunteer, "I don't want to eat chicken because then I'll know what it tastes like and then I will always want it. It's better not to know." Some kids have put food in their clothes to take home to their families.

After lunch they have more teaching and instruction. Then there is football (known as soccer in the United States). The competition is fierce: the prize is the coveted Mama Maggie Cup!

They eat dinner. They pray. They play Ping-Pong, a game at which Mama Maggie excelled at in her youth. They laugh and cry together, they plan together, and they get a taste of a life—the happy life of a child—that they have never known.

They sleep in clean beds, their stomachs full, dreaming new dreams.

Mama Maggie once asked a girl attending a camp, "What do you dream of?"

The girl could not quite comprehend the question. "Nothing," she said.

"What?" Mama Maggie persisted.

The child thought carefully. "I dream of a piece of tomato."

At camp, the children's dreams—and their confidence—get bigger, because they realize they are in a safe place.

Joe Cope, the DC businessman, visited one of the camps. He was sitting in the back of the room with three other foreign visitors during a big group session with hundreds of kids. All the children were singing, laughing, and generally absorbing so much good stuff that they had almost gotten physically bigger over the course of the camp.

One little boy, about five years old, had been horribly burned on the face after an accident with a kerosene lamp in his slum home. When he arrived at camp, at first he cowered in corners and slunk on the sidelines, ashamed of his scars.

But during this group session, Joe says, that little boy was on the front row, smiling and singing with everyone else. Suddenly, while everyone else was seated, he stood up. His counselors stared as he slowly made his way down the center aisle to the back of the room.

He approached Joe, looked him right in the eyes, and, grinning big, extended his hand. He carefully shook hands with each of the four foreign visitors, then, having properly welcomed them, made his way back to his seat.

One year a bus driver who happened to be Muslim had been hired to transport the kids to camp. Three days later he arrived to take them back to the slum. "I could not believe it," he told Youssef. "On the way to the camp, the kids were impossible. They were yelling. They were rude and vulgar. On the way back home, they were like little angels. I could not believe they were the same kids!"

For some kids, particularly boys, camp is an opportunity to give up things they thought they wanted. In the garbage villages, young boys assert their manhood by smoking, doing drugs, and sexually abusing kids younger than themselves. By the end of each camp session, Mama Maggie typically ends up with dozens of packs of cigarettes presented to her by eight-year-old boys, as well as all kinds of other paraphernalia that the kids surrender to her in hopes of starting a new life.

MAMA MAGGIE ALWAYS ASKS THE STAFF TO GIVE HER THE most difficult children, the most uncooperative ones who just aren't going to give up anything. One of these boys was named Ramzi. He was a teenager who absolutely did not want to listen to anyone.

The first year Ramzi came to camp he was a very tough adolescent.

Ditto the second year. In the end, he came to five camps over three years, and every year he was worse than before. Staff members said to Maggie, "Mama, don't waste your time!"

He seemed like a hopeless case. Still, everyone kept praying for Ramzi. They poured their love into him, hugged him, and included him in everything they did at camp. There would be small break-throughs: He kept repenting. He was really sorry about how bad he was. But he could or would not change.

Nothing was happening, or so they thought.

And then a few years later, after Ramzi aged out of the program, when Mama Maggie was thinking about anything else but Ramzi, she went to her quiet, empty church before dawn. She saw a young man near the front, standing in a corner, reading the Bible and earnestly, humbly praying. It was Ramzi.

Chapter 19

The Dark Side and the Light

*If we could read the secret history of our enemies, we would find in
each person's life sorrow and suffering enough to disarm all hostility.*

—Henry Wadsworth Longfellow

AT THE CAMPS, SHOCKING PERSONAL STORIES OF THE KIDS come forth. Hunger, thirst, dirt, disease, and poverty are bad enough. But the most intractable evils Mama Maggie and her coworkers deal with have to do with sexual and physical abuse. These blights are found at every socioeconomic level. But they are wretchedly concentrated in the areas where Stephen's Children works.

Some children have no idea that being raped is wrong. One little girl at camp, for example, told a staff worker that her father often came to her at night. She didn't know there was anything unusual about that; all she knew was that it hurt. She was gently told that the next time it started, she should tell her father, "No! It hurts me!"

She did, and reported back to her leader that her father broke down and cried.

Another little girl's story came out when she was at camp, learning about God, "our Father, who art in heaven," as the Lord's Prayer puts it. She jumped up and ran away from her small group. A staff worker followed her. "If my earthly father [abuses] me," she cried, "why would I want a heavenly Father?"

Female staff members comforted her, cared for her, and confronted the earthly dad. The abuse stopped.

A CHEERFUL, DARK-HAIRED WOMAN NAMED SOFIA HAS DEALT with such challenges over twenty years of working with Stephen's Children.

Sofia was a teacher in a primary school before she came to work with Mama Maggie, and she loved her job, but something was missing. She wasn't sure what.

One day she was in church, alone, crying and praying. She was thinking about what seemed to be missing in her life, great as it was. Then she saw a small advertisement posted for a job with Stephen's Children. She felt compelled to interview for the position.

She was taken to a slum. "The first thing that attracted me was the simplicity of the poor children and families," she says today. "They really needed someone to come to them. They couldn't go out and find help. They were way below the poverty line, but they were so happy to know that someone cared about them and that I would come to *listen* to them, not just read the Bible or give them food and then leave right away."

Sofia says she learned from Mama Maggie how to set goals and organize her life, but mostly how to really listen to people. "Maybe I can't solve all their problems, but the main thing is that they know I am really listening to them. I learned that from Mama Maggie listening to me."

Listening is a hallmark trait of the people around Mama Maggie. In their conversations, you never hear the polite but disingenuous phrase, "Well, now let me let you go," which generally means, "*I* need to go now." Many of the habitual hustles in the West are missing in the East. There, people make time. They connect. They converse. They might be late to the next appointment, and the one after that, but no matter. They are fully present, not just focused on getting to the next thing.

In that mode, Sofia would spend hours helping girls with their homework, encouraging them to set goals, laughing with them, and crying with them when she heard their hard stories. One girl had a heart problem, but her main fear was of her father, who would harass and attack her sexually. She had no birth certificate, no official papers to prove she existed. She was no one.

Through the ministry, Sofia was able to help the girl get official papers, and even heart surgery. But the main healing came when she got a leader from the church to intervene with the girl's father. There was repentance, forgiveness, a new beginning, and healing.

Many years later Sofia was at a bus stop and heard someone calling her name. It was that little girl, now grown up into a beautiful young woman. "Remember me?" she said. "I'm married now. I am well!"

A MAN NAMED AMIN HAS BEEN WITH STEPHEN'S CHILDREN for fourteen years. He worked with a boy named Guirguis. Guirguis was fifteen years old, uneducated, insolent, and aggressive. He regularly raped his younger sister. "We would just write him off," Amin says. "But Mama Maggie doesn't write off anyone."

Guirguis came to a camp. He was sitting in a small group with other guys his age. Stephen's Children leaders are trained to bring up difficult subjects, and the leader began to gently address the issue of sexual abuse.

Guirguis, the last person anyone would ever suppose would have a conscience, suddenly began to weep uncontrollably. He confessed to the group what he had been doing. He told them how he never felt anything from other people except fear and loathing. "People always just tell me, 'Oh, you're going to be locked up in prison,'" he said. "But here in this camp, I have seen how people care about me. *Me!*"

With Guirguis's mother's permission, the female leaders took the younger sister away from her dangerous home. They gave her a safe place to live and helped her begin to heal from her dark memories of abuse. Amin and other male leaders got permission to relocate Guirguis as well. They found a job for him in a monastery, where he worked hard, felt compassion, and submitted himself to God for a cure from his destructive ways.

Today Guirguis and his sister are both grown and happily married. Their former life in the garbage seems like a bad dream.

A TWELVE-YEAR-OLD BOY CALLED MINA HAD AN ELDER brother and uncle who both raped him. His father was addicted to hashish and out of his mind most of the time. The brother and uncle would hang the boy from a rusty iron beam and beat him.

This terrible story came out in camp. Mama Maggie's staff found a safe place for the boy to live. When they visited his home to see what they could do there, the elder brother attacked them. He is now in prison, and Mina was able to grow up safely.

And then there is ten-year-old Anthony, the boy introduced in the opening chapter of this book, the boy who had been burned and abused, then rescued and given new beginnings by Mama Maggie.

Stephen's Children helped Anthony get a new birth certificate and the identity papers that had been lost in the chaos of his young childhood. Since he had dropped out of school to work at such a young age, he could not return. Mama Maggie's staff gave him educational and vocational training, and today he has graduated from high school and has a new life. "I don't know what my future would have been if someone did not care enough to love me," he says.

— *Chapter 20* —

God's Athletes

Although the life of a person is in a land full of thorns and weeds, there is always a space in which the good seed can grow. You have to trust God.

—Pope Francis

The highest form of worship is the worship of unselfish . . . service. The greatest form of praise is the sound of consecrated feet seeking out the lost and helpless.

—Billy Graham

MAMA MAGGIE FILLS HER SPIRITUAL FUEL TANK THROUGH daily meditation and prayers at three o'clock in the morning. She also makes time to remove herself from the hectic pace of the work to the solitude of the desert for refreshment.

The work of running a charity could easily be all-consuming. In spite of the fact that she has a gifted, committed team all around her—people like her husband, her brothers, Youssef, Dr. Abraam, Kristina, and so many others—the work could gobble up all of Mama Maggie's time and attention, all day, every day.

But Mama Maggie has been wise enough to pull herself away from the daily demands of the effort, important as it is. She realizes she needs time alone in order to nurture her soul so she can best serve the children of the slums and set an example and atmosphere for her staff. She also knows that she is not indispensable.

So she often goes to the desert.

Members of Mama Maggie's extended family outside of Egypt laugh when they think about her contemplative life. Not that there is anything amusing about going to the monastery to meditate . . . they just tease her and love how Mama Maggie improvises when she's in the fast-paced culture of the United States.

Years ago Mama Maggie came to the Washington, DC, area, where her daughter, Ann, was spending time with family. Mama Maggie's sister, brother-in-law, nieces, nephews, and all kinds of extended family members were there as well. Mama Maggie was staying in a condominium in the same building as her sister.

The family shared many meals, conversations, and much laughter. There was a mystery, however. Periodically, Maggie would turn up missing.

One day Mama Maggie's nephew Mark went looking for her. He went into the master bedroom and opened a closet door. There was his aunt, lying prone on her face in the dark closet, praying.

"Come out," he called. "What are you doing?"

Other family members appeared, crowding into the bedroom. "Come out! Why aren't you being with us?"

Despite the entreaties from her family, Maggie would not emerge until she was ready.

During that visit, whenever the family couldn't find Mama Maggie, they knew she was lying on the floor in the closet, meditating.

While not particularly normal behavior, it is evidence of something powerful going on inside of Mama Maggie. When asked about this, as in "Why were you in the closet?" she smiled and said, "I'm praying for all of you!"

The condo closet is a far cry from the ancient, windswept monasteries of Egypt, which is where Mama Maggie goes for solitude, prayer, and meditation when she's in her own country. As she says, it is crucial to do this, wherever you are. In her words, it's always good to take time to:

Silence your tongue to listen to your thoughts.

Silence your thought to listen to your heart beating.

Silence your heart to listen to your spirit.

And silence your spirit, to listen to His spirit.

MAMA MAGGIE'S COUNTRY WAS THE BIRTHPLACE OF A NEW, contemplative mode of life back in the second century. Its deserts are vast; over the centuries, many monks went out to seek God in the solitude, sanctuary, and arid challenges of the sands. These men are known in history as the Desert Fathers. There is also a lesser-known band of Desert Mothers, as God and the desert give equal opportunity for both genders.

Collectively, they were all also known as "God's athletes"—vigorous, disciplined people who often did what seemed physically impossible. They denied themselves the normal needs of the body. They focused on a life of humility, prayer, and communion with God. They lived in caves. And even though the earliest of the desert contemplatives lived almost two thousand years ago, Egypt's contemporary Copts like Mama Maggie feel a connection with them as if these hearty men and women lived yesterday, and still live today.

One of the earliest people to go to the desert was a man named Antony, or Anthony, or Antonius. Born to a wealthy family in Lower Egypt in about AD 251, he lost both his parents at a young age and was due to come into a large inheritance. There are various stories about what happened next.

In one, he heard a sermon about renouncing wealth and worldly possessions, and determined to do so. In another version of the story, he watched a funeral procession pass by one day, and took to heart the fact that the wealthy man who had died was leaving this world empty-handed. He was just a body wrapped in a shroud. No properties, possessions, or exalted position. Why hold on to money and material things, Antony reasoned, when you would eventually leave this life with nothing?

In another version of the story, Antony's brother contested the inheritance; so Antony decided to give the money to his sibling and seek a different sort of life.

Regardless of how he disposed of his income, the end result was that he was no longer encumbered by worldly possessions. He renounced his former life and went into the desert, one of the first of many contemplatives who would follow Jesus' pattern of going into the wilderness to focus on God and depend on his words to defeat temptations. He found a place to live, a tiny cave in the rocky hills 450 feet above the sands.

So Antony dwelt in solitude and the arid beauty of the Egyptian desert. Late in his life, he discovered, to his surprise, that he was not alone, that there was another recluse who had also come to this difficult place to draw closer to God.

His name was Paul; the monastery built in his honor is on the other side of the mountain from Antony's.

These ancient monks, and many like them, settled in solitary places to connect with God. Some went to be alone and were surprised that seekers and spiritual pilgrims tracked them down, wanting to learn from them. Their cells and caves in the desert became pilgrimage destinations for Christians throughout the Roman Empire. They built communities of both silence and fellowship and shared meals, work, and faith. Some produced some of the most significant writings in the history of Christianity. Others were illiterate and lived unrecorded lives of faith and prayer. The most famous of them were known as "Stars of the Egyptian Desert."

To profile the movement most simply, there were three forms of monasticism in the deserts of Egypt. There were monks who lived isolated for decades, communing only with God. Others lived in solitary cells but gathered corporately for worship and counsel. In the third form, believers would live together in a monastic complex, sharing meals, prayer, work, and rest.

Today, if you drive north of Cairo on the highway heading to the east and take a turn when you hit the Red Sea, you will arrive at one of the oldest active monasteries in the world. It is dedicated to Saint Antony.

If you are fortunate enough to come here with Mama Maggie, you will find that this—and other monasteries in the desert—are spiritual homes for her, the places where she feels, perhaps, most in touch with God. (Because of her contemplative times here, she also feels him in the chaos of the slums, the garbage, and the most unlovely places as well.)

But here in the monastery, Mama Maggie walks the grounds, smiling and picking up small stones warmed by the desert sun. She tucks them in her pocket. She smiles at the dry mountains and the deep-blue skies. She connects with her spiritual father, Abouna Fanous, a priest in his late eighties who is in poor health, teetering on the outskirts of heaven. The monks of the monastery bring him from his cell in his wheelchair. Mama Maggie feeds him by hand. He asks for each visitor's name. He prays over each one.

He prayed specifically for a friend back in the United States, a young woman named Ashley. At that time she was dying, in desperate need of a liver transplant she might well not live to receive. Today she has a new liver, from a living donor, and enjoys new health.

Much like Mama Maggie herself, Abouna Fanous is an intriguing blend of down-to-earth practicality and otherworldliness. He laughs and says delightful, implausible things. He doesn't emerge from his cell very often, but when he does, monastery visitors run to him and mob his wheelchair, kissing his hands, asking him to bless their children.

To someone who has never been to a monastery, its ancient habits and its many long-deceased monks enshrined in wall niches may feel a bit foreign. But it's a place of rich, deep hospitality. It is one of what have been called the "thin places" on the planet, a physical place where any open person, from any background, might well sense the palpable heritage of generations of people meditating upon God.

The bearded monks there, wearing long black cassocks, traditional bonnet-like hats, and carrying their cell phones, are most charming. They will show you artwork drawn by their counterparts in the fourth century, carefully restored by archaeologists. (In 2002, the Egyptian government initiated an eight-year project to restore the monastery and its works of art.) Scholars have called this monastery the "Coptic Sistine chapel."[1] It shows the development of centuries of distinctly Egyptian Christian art.

If you visit there, you'll see the new church under construction on the grounds. It's full of scaffolding, building materials, and Egyptian pigeons. The bright colors painted in detailed murals on the ceiling are breathtaking, as are the intricate designs of the many stained glass windows.

You might look up at the colored glass figures and patterns illuminated by the powerful desert sun, their colors refracting like bright prisms on the unfinished floor of the church. If you were to ask, "Who did this?" here's the shy response you might get from your host: "I did. I was an interior designer before I became a monk."

You'll also see the places where, in earlier centuries, the monks had to build escape routes and secure defenses because of constant attacks from invaders. The monastery is serene today, even though its monks are mindful of the burning and destruction of monasteries and convents in their own country, as well as next-door country Syria and other volatile parts of the Middle East.

Mama Maggie loves this place. She spends hours and sometimes days in solitude, meditation, and prayer, and then returns home with fresh vision and vigor to the poor people in the slums and her staff who serve them.

It's also a place where Mama Maggie has gone on several occasions when she's been waiting for a certain type of news that few can relate to.

FOR THE HANDFUL OF PEOPLE ON THE PLANET WHO ARE nominated each year for the Nobel Peace Prize, the beginning of October is a time of waiting and wondering. Nominees know that they will in due course receive a phone call from Europe with the news if they have won the famous prize and its purse of more than a million dollars. Or not. For Mama Maggie—and presumably other nominees as well—the anticipation is much more difficult for her friends than for her.

Kristina, her friend and staff member, describes how recently when Mama Maggie and a group of friends from her team had gone to the St. Mary's monastery in Assiut, about five hundred kilometers south of Cairo. The winner of the Nobel was just about to be announced. Mama Maggie had begun to receive a lot of media attention throughout Egypt and the world. For some predictors of the prize, she was the heavy favorite—not that the Nobel Peace Prize is a horse race. A media team was on its way to the monastery to record interviews and reactions after the announcement.

Mama Maggie walked the grounds of the monastery, watching the birds, listening to the palm trees rustle in the wind, and picking up stones, smiling as she tucked them in her pocket. Eventually the phone call came. The Nobel had, in fact, been awarded that year to the European Union.

"It's okay," responded Mama Maggie once Kristina found her sitting on the floor in one of the many chapels on the grounds. "I'm not sad, don't you be sad!" She smiled in her characteristic way, almost like a child, and sang a simple song, a song about being thankful in every situation. It was as if time stood still for her, and she was in a place beyond normal human hopes for fame and fortune.

"It wasn't that she was indifferent," Kristina says. "She wasn't removed or in denial. She was ready to give a statement for the media. But she was absolutely at peace. It was a big lesson to me about getting to the place in your life where you just don't feel disappointment, no matter what happens."

The media crew arrived at the monastery. They found Mama Maggie taking a sunny walk with her husband, Ibrahim. The director of the media team, Mariam, says that she kept looking for signs of disappointment in Mama Maggie.

"But all I saw," she says, "was joy. She was in the hands of someone who knew best and who did the best for all his children. Mama Maggie would leave us for moments to go check on or feed Amaal, an elderly paraplegic woman who she had been caring for and had brought with her to the monastery. It was surreal."

The extended group had lunch together in the compound. Some of the staff members like Youssef had tears of disappointment running down their faces. Mama Maggie stood on her tiptoes and wiped them away.

"Over lunch," Mariam says, "Mama Maggie talked about new projects for the children, new permits for a new center, new visions, new hopes. She lifted up the morale of her entire team, not in an artificial or pretentious way, but sincerely.

"It was as if she was celebrating a different kind of winning. Mama Maggie and the children were winners because they were chosen and blessed to serve for a greater recognition—to serve the poor. The Nobel was irrelevant. She showed the freedom and surrender of someone who knew that she was in God's heart. Nothing else seemed to matter."

Chapter 21

The Next Generation

If you are not yet wise enough, walk with the wise.
If you are not a saint yet, live with saints. Walk
with those who have a candle, in their light.

—Mama Maggie

IN THE FIRST TWENTY YEARS OF HER WORK IN THE POOR villages, Mama Maggie was in the slums, all day, every day. Today, while she loves the children and families no less, she hears another call. It's counterintuitive in the sense that most visionaries keep their hands on the wheel of the work they've started for as long as possible, as if the work can only thrive in their presence.

Mama Maggie has consciously pulled back. She trusts the people who have joined her staff. She trusts that God is guiding this work. She knows it's not all about her. She goes to the desert, to the monasteries, where she touches the ancient stones, wonders at the star-filled skies, and is well aware of the transient nature of life on earth.

"I'm only beginning to know how small I am," she says. "There are 7 billion people in the world. Think of all the stars in the heavens, the galaxies! We are small! Yet when the Almighty is there, any little human can have a lot of meaning in history."

This may well be the key to Mama Maggie's boldness in dreaming big dreams for her ministry. It is also the key to her humility.

Meanwhile, young women and men are stepping up, the next generation of compassionate people who are serving the poor.

For example, Eriny, a beautiful extrovert, leads the children in singing and teaching at one of the community centers. She constantly encourages the children—many who struggle with deep-seated inferiority—by telling them that they are gifted, talented, and loved. Eriny is particularly equipped to spread that message, for she has lived the life of many of the kids she leads.

She came from one of these poor neighborhoods. She had seven brothers and one sister. Her brothers treated her as an inferior, stupid girl. Her mother was distant, more occupied with the boys. Eriny was shy and insecure, best able to express herself in writing.

When she was a young teen, other girls recognized her writing gift. They asked her to write letters to their boyfriends. When they told her what they wanted her to write, she was uncomfortable. But she wanted them to like her and couldn't say no.

Somehow, one of the risqué letters got into the hands of Eriny's brother. "This is your handwriting!" he yelled at her. "You're having a bad relationship with this boy!" He knocked her around and told her mother, who started yelling and beating her.

This was the most attention Eriny had ever received from her mom.

Eriny went to church that night, weeping. She prayed, "Where are you, God?" She sensed him drawing near to her, caring for her when no one else did.

Eriny continued into her teens feeling shy, insecure, and afraid of people. Then a girl at her school went to a Stephen's Children camp and could not stop talking about how much she enjoyed it. By now Eriny was seventeen, too old to be served by Mama Maggie's staff. She was curious and decided she would volunteer to help, even though she knew nothing about it.

During her interview, Eriny was terrified. She thought the ministry wouldn't take her. It was so hard for her to talk with people. But the interviewers were encouraging. "You're very clever," they told her. "You can be a great help to us."

Eriny had never in her life heard such simple words of encouragement.

By the time she met Mama Maggie, she had heard all about her, yet nothing had prepared her for the sense of power and love and joy she felt from this woman. "I felt like everything she said was just for me alone," Eriny says. "I felt like Mama Maggie knew what I was thinking. I felt like she could be the mother I'd always wanted."

Eriny began to come out of her sad shell, but she was still living in her troubled home at the time. During a three-day camp, she and the other leaders were meeting with Mama Maggie. "Someone wants to say something to me," Mama Maggie said. "Go ahead and say it, right away!"

Tears rolled down Eriny's face. "I love it here," she said. "I don't want to go back home."

Mama Maggie looked at her. It was as if she could see Eriny's heart. "May I visit you at your home?" she asked.

Eriny couldn't answer, she says, because she was so full of joy.

But once she got back home, time went by, and she assumed Mama Maggie had forgotten about her. Then she got a phone call from a staff member who knew her. "Mama Maggie will be at your home in two hours," she said.

Eriny's mother lived in a small apartment, and one of her brothers lived upstairs with his wife. He was a nervous, aggressive man who was alienated from everyone. Though a gifted artist, he had failed at everything he'd ever attempted professionally. And he and his wife had been trying to have children for years, to no avail.

Eriny wanted to explain all of the complex and troubled family dynamics to Mama Maggie, but Mama stopped her. "Don't tell me," she said. "I will go visit with each one."

Eriny's mother was full of bitterness because of the estrangement from her son. Mama Maggie listened patiently, then told her, "He will be all right. Today, in fact, he will come and give you a hug and a kiss."

Then Mama Maggie went to see the man. She admired his paintings. "I will buy these from you," she said. "I can use them in our camps." She gave him money on the spot, which he could use to repay his debts. They prayed together, and then Mama Maggie told him, "I'll pray you will have a daughter soon . . . and her name will be Mary."

The young man came downstairs with Mama Maggie, went to his mom's apartment, and apologized to his mother for his bad behavior and alienation. She held out her arms, and they hugged and kissed.

And yes, nine months after that visit, the son and his wife had a baby girl. They named her Mary.

"Mama Maggie has taught me that love is for everyone," Eriny says, who is now married and has a small child. "I felt her love, and now I can talk in front of a crowd of people, I can express my feelings to everyone. I go to the slums, and I want the girls there to know what I have learned. So many of them are on the verge of losing their way; they just need someone to listen to them. I can show them that there is hope for change for them . . . like I changed."

IN A VERY DIFFERENT CONTEXT, COMING FROM A CHILD-hood of wealth rather than poverty, a background of big dreams rather than no dreams, another member of a new generation has changed a lot as well. He is Amir, Mama Maggie and Ibrahim's only son.

Amir, like his sister, Ann, grew up in this upper-class family whose members loved one anther, loved God, and loved the poor.

Amir, like his brilliant father, excelled in school. He was consistently first in everything. He went to a private Jesuit school where his classmates were the sons of presidents.

He asked to go to a military boarding school in the United States: "I want the discipline."

He received his undergraduate engineering education at the American University of Cairo and earned his MBA in France. He then worked at the Deutschland bank in London and lived in Manhattan as an investment banker.

He was also, like his mom, a great person to hang out with. A friend says, "When I wanted to have fun, I'd connect with Amir." He remembers riding on the hood of Amir's car at a high rate of speed, laughing in the desert breeze.

Even as Amir lived the fun, privileged, successful, New York-London-Paris-Cairo lifestyle, he was always tied to the poor. He did all kinds of charitable work. He met with ministry leaders who were spearheading relief initiatives. He constantly connected with his mother's staff and their work. His friends admired him for his knowledge of both wealth and poverty.

And then, not unlike his mother, at a time of life when many young professionals press on, intent on acquiring more, the next big deal, the next new achievement, he paused. In 2013, Amir went to a quiet place to think and pray.

And then, on his own volition, surprising everyone who knew him, and his family most of all, Amir sold all his properties and his luxury possessions. He worked out a power of attorney with his dad in order to take care of things. *What is life for?* he thought. He decided to enter the monastic life, taking on vows of chastity, poverty, and obedience.

Amir's decision was like an "earthquake," Mama Maggie says. It shook everybody up.

But as an investment expert and a strategic thinker, Amir had been around the world and around the block, so to speak. He had seen most everything that successful people in his position could, and did what they could enjoy. He had hit all the prestigious marks someone in his field might strive for. And yet he decided to change paths, to invest his life in an entirely different way.

---- *Chapter 22* ----

Lives Touching Lives

. . . all that I am and all that I have, the faculties of my mind,
the members of my body, my worldly possessions, my time, and
my influence over others, all to be used entirely for Thy glory
and resolutely employed in obedience to Thy commands.

—Thomas Maclellan's family covenant, June 7, 1857

FRANCES HEALD IS ANOTHER YOUNG PERSON WHOSE LIFE bears the mentoring marks of Mama Maggie's influence. Frances grew up in a place as far from Cairo's slums as you could imagine.

Lookout Mountain, Tennessee, is a suburb of Chattanooga. Almost 40 percent of its residents can be considered wealthy—by local standards, let alone the rest of the world—compared to 4 percent in the rest of Tennessee. Rolling green mountains stand over the peaceful valley below, where horses run in white-fenced fields. Civil War statues and bronze cannons dot the landscape.

Lookout Mountain is also a bastion of Reformed Presbyterians. Their flagship college, Covenant, sits on top of the mountain. It is full of thoughtful students who look to John Calvin and other such thinkers for their religious perspective. The local Presbyterian churches are full. It's safe to assume that the Coptic population on the mountain is scarce.

Growing up in this insular environment, Frances could have been rather parochial. But she comes from a family in which her parents and grandparents on both sides have radically emphasized the notion that real faith in God expresses itself in a certain generosity of lifestyle. Like Mama Maggie, they believe that faith reveals itself in caring for those who have had the misfortune to be born in dark and difficult places.

By the time Frances was seven years old, her parents, Daryl and Cathy Heald, had taught her to split her allowance into three envelopes: "Giving," "Saving," and "Spending." If the family went out to eat, her dad would offer the kids the choice to order Sprite or water to drink with their meal. If they ordered water, he'd give the money they would have spent on the soft drink to charity. Choosing to give to those with less was elemental to the Heald household.

By the time Frances was a teenager, she had been to twenty-five countries around the world. These were not exotic resorts and European tours. Frances traveled with her dad to visit relief and development work in places like Ethiopia, Cambodia, India, Peru, and Thailand, to name a few.

During Frances's first trip to India, when she was ten, she saw a toddler sitting on the dirty sidewalk, covered with a newspaper. There was no attentive mother or caring dad keeping watch over her. She was alone.

When Frances was twelve, she traveled with her dad to Mumbai and its notorious red-light district. Daryl was working in conjunction with International Justice Mission, which rescues children from sex trafficking and slavery and brings justice to their oppressors.[1] Frances stared through the windows of their vehicle as they made their way slowly down a street clogged with motorbikes, street hawkers, and lots of ambling men. She saw a girl her own age in a storefront window. The girl had dark eyes, long black hair, no expression on her face. There were bars over the glass as she looked out at the street. This twelve-year-old was a prostitute.

By the time she was in eighth grade, Frances had seen deeply disturbing scenes like the ones in India all over the world. But she had also seen how their horrors could be dissipated by caring people who brought hope to the dark places. She knew from her parents that one day God would ultimately set everything right that was so wrong. She also saw that people following his ways could make a significant difference here and now.

"Returning to the safety of home on Lookout Mountain became the hardest part of traveling," Frances says. It was hard to hang out with teenaged friends who just wanted to chat and go to Starbucks, without a clue how the rest of the world lived. Her heart ached for the people she'd seen in the slums and villages. She felt guilty that she lived in comfort and safety when they were suffering and vulnerable. Though she gradually realized that brokenness is everywhere—her upscale girlfriend was broken with the pain she internalized over her parents' divorce, for example—Frances felt more drawn to work among the poor and help however she could.

Then one night Frances doubled over in pain. Her parents rushed her to the local emergency room. Tests for everything doctors could think of came back negative. Weeks, then months, then years went by. It only got worse: Frances's bones hurt so badly that she sometimes could not get out of bed. Her muscles knotted. Her brain felt like it was going to explode with fever. Sometimes her fatigue was so intense that walking across the room felt overwhelming.

Some of the many doctors she saw inferred it might all be in her head. It was progressively infuriating, as were some of the well-meaning and kind comments from family friends.

"The last thing I wanted was for 'God's strength to be made perfect in my weakness,'" Frances says, mentioning an often-quoted Bible verse about suffering. "I felt like I was young and strong, and I could handle this."

But as the years went by, her body got weaker, her anger got stronger, and her condition became chronic.

Why would God show me so many terrible needs around the world, she wondered, thinking about her travels to poor places, *and then allow me to have this physical problem so I can't do anything about them?*

One evening, when Frances was sixteen, her parents held a dinner gathering for a ministry worker visiting from another nation. This often happened; the Heald home was a center of international briefings and lively gatherings of every sort.

That visitor was Mama Maggie. She told the large group about what she was doing in the poor areas of Cairo. Frances doesn't remember just how it happened, but at some point in the evening, the lady in white came to talk with her where she was sitting on the fringes of the group. It was as if Mama Maggie had some special frequency for her pain and had picked it up from across the crowded room.

They went to another part of the house, just the two of them. Frances wasn't sure why, but she found herself spilling everything out, her anger, her pain, her confusion, her depression. Mama Maggie listened. She pointed Frances toward some verses about hope. She talked about real hope, that it's not dependent on God healing your physical problem. She also anointed Frances's head with oil—an ancient biblical practice—and prayed tenderly for her, first in English, then in Arabic. Mama Maggie wasn't a miracle worker. But she was a good listener through whom God's love came to Frances.

"I realized that sometimes spiritual and emotional healings are the greatest healing we can receive," Frances says. "It was such a release. I cried the rest of the night, just holding Mama Maggie's hand; she kept me by her side wherever she went." To her shock, for the first time since she'd gotten sick, Frances felt some sense of peace.

Mama Maggie returned to Egypt but kept in touch with Frances.

The conversation that night was a tipping point. "My prayers during that time were not pretty," Frances says. "But slowly my pride began to fall away. I told God that if he wanted to do something with my life, he could, but I had given up trying to manage it. I wasn't in control anymore.

"I'm not sure how he does it, but through all my angry prayers, God drew me closer to him."

Right around the same time as Mama Maggie's visit, Frances was finally diagnosed. It was Lyme disease. This ailment is a lot more common in temperate parts of the United States than it used to be; it's caused by tick bites that transmit a bacterium that causes severe reactions. If undiagnosed, as in Frances's case, the infection spreads to joints, the heart, and the nervous system. For some time, antibiotics did help her, but then became not only ineffective but harmful. So, barring some miracle, she'll deal with episodes of pain and fatigue the rest of her life.

Around two years after Mama Maggie's visit to her home, after her illness had been brought under control, Frances traveled with her dad and a number of friends from their church to see the work of Mama Maggie and her staff in Cairo. Frances played with the street children, visited their programs, listened to them sing and recite verses, and then Mama Maggie came to her and asked if they could talk privately. She asked how Frances had been feeling; she talked with her about not losing hope. She prayed for her again, in both English and Arabic, and gave her a small cross. "Remember," she whispered as she hugged Frances good-bye, "our ultimate hope is in the ultimate healing we will one day have in Christ!"

Today, Frances points to many influences that have shaped her life and character: her faith, family, travels, illness, her parents' adoption—after much nice nagging and begging by Frances and her sister,

Hallie—of three young Chinese siblings with special needs, and so many more relationships, experiences, challenges, and surprises.

These, as well as Mama Maggie's influence, also led her to go to nursing school. Now in her early twenties, Frances is a cardiovascular intensive care nurse at a children's hospital in Alabama. The children she cares for each day have congenital heart defects or have had heart transplants or other serious cardiac issues.

"One thing that has helped me in my nursing career," she says, "was seeing Mama Maggie washing the slum kids' feet. They were covered with scabs, thick with dirt, calloused and sore. When she was with a group, Mama Maggie would always focus first on the least, and then perhaps make her way to the more 'important' people. I try to do the same thing in my work; I look to see those in the room who might be considered 'unimportant.'

"I also learned this from Mama Maggie: She said that Jesus didn't need her. He *allowed* her to participate with him in his ways. So washing kids' feet was a privilege. For me, I realized that he doesn't need me, but I get to participate in his work. My working with him and for him is a privilege for me, not a necessity for him. It gives me a passion for life and the people around me that nothing else could."

Chapter 23

Real Love

We have been called to heal wounds, to unite what has fallen apart, and to bring home those who have lost their way.

—Francis of Assisi

In December 2008, Frances Heald's father, Daryl, took a group of his friends to visit Mama Maggie's work in Cairo. It was a group that included a number of wealthy individuals. These were people who could likely become donors to the poor families. Daryl had seen the usual dynamic before: whenever he brought potential supporters to visit a charitable work in a needy nation, the charity would usually welcome the guests with much ado, putting forward the best face possible in order to garner support.

But when Daryl brought his group of about twenty well-to-do individuals to the camp complex in Mokattam, Mama Maggie was nowhere to be seen. They were told she was on her way.

Members of the group visited with the staff and played with the dozens of children roaming the courtyard . . . and then Mama Maggie arrived.

She did not greet the expectant wealthy visitors. Instead, she went straight to her spigot and washbasin. A line of small, filthy children quickly assembled. Mama Maggie quietly began washing their feet and trimming their toenails. She took her time with each one, asking his or her name, finding out what they thought about, worried about, and loved.

"It's not like she was rude," Daryl says. "It's just that she doesn't do anything the usual way."

Daryl himself is a fairly unusual person. He's been to seventy countries around the world. In order to determine wise funding grants for a charity foundation, he has reviewed hundreds of charitable works among the poor all over the planet. He says that the programs of Mama Maggie are similar to other such efforts. Many worthy charities care for the needy and equip people to break the cycle of poverty.

But Daryl also says that there is something unique about Stephen's Children and the work they do. It has to do with Mama Maggie's character and the environment she creates in the most unlikely places.

"Leaders define cultures," Daryl says. "She brings peace to a place of utter chaos in the slums. The Holy Spirit is in her, and his power. She has authority. She doesn't need to raise her voice. She has real love. Other non-government organizations are doing lots of good things, but Mama Maggie's work has deep *quality*, not just quantity."

Mama Maggie and her workers don't try to impress visitors. No one, including Mama Maggie or her leaders, seems to have a business card. They do use, however, simple tools—time and sweat—to show love to kids and families.

For example, a little boy named Paul lives in a small village in Upper Egypt. His father, a farmer, had hit very hard times. Paul's shack had no toilet. The family had to dispose of waste by the side of a canal in the village. They were embarrassed and harassed by neighbors who were of a different faith.

Paul told his special friend from Stephen's Children about the problem. Ever practical, the leader came to the home and made a case study. He prayed with the family, visiting often, telling them that God cared even about their most basic needs.

Stephen's Children workers built a toilet, with a door that could close. They finished it as quickly as they could. In the simple words of one worker: "The family now feels more secure and happy to be more like normal human beings. They also know that their heavenly Father sends them help and never forgets them. Now they can trust God who provides solutions to their problems through people like the workers of Mama Maggie."

It is one thing to build a toilet for a poor family. It is another for the toilet to become a tangible emblem of the love of God.

Part of Mama Maggie's power, paradoxically, comes from the fact that she gave up a "powerful" lifestyle. As noted earlier, before her work in the slums, and before she became a simple woman in white, she was an impressive force.

"She was an attractive, wealthy, global businesswoman," Daryl says. "But she allowed love to change her. The successful type-A personalities appreciate that. They see that her work isn't a dog and pony show or a personality cult. People are attracted to truth. Mama Maggie seeks out brokenness. She doesn't 'do' ministry. She *is* ministry."

Matt Jacoby, who came into Mama Maggie's large, extended Egyptian family by marrying Maggie's niece Maria, agrees. But he expresses the idea in a different, and pretty radical, way.

"Mama Maggie is the best picture of Jesus that I've ever met."

Matt first met Mama Maggie during one of her U.S. visits, when he and Maria were young Washington, DC, professionals and dating. Maria had told him stories about this aunt who wears a white T-shirt, works with the poor, and has been nominated for the Nobel Peace Prize. Matt met Maggie at a big family gathering in the DC suburbs. The family grilled steaks, talked, laughed, and had a casual, fun dinner.

As Matt was leaving, Mama Maggie held both his hands and told him good-bye. He went down the front steps of the home, toward his car, and then sensed she had followed him. She had made no noise.

He noticed something out of the corner of his eye and turned around. There she was, sitting on the steps, just looking at him. Thinking. Praying, perhaps.

Later, as sometimes happens, Matt and Maria had to work out some things in their relationship, and they broke up. It was a hard time.

Eight months into the breakup, Mama Maggie was visiting in the United States again. She came with Maria to her place of worship, a huge church near DC, with multiple satellite campuses. It's about as far from Mama Maggie's ancient Coptic roots as one could possibly imagine.

Matt saw Mama Maggie in the lobby. She knew of his pain in the breakup. She came to him and gave him a hug, then held both his hands in hers and looked him in the eyes.

"I tell you," she said. "One day I'm going to hold your children— the ones you have with Maria—in my arms."

Matt didn't know what to think, but he felt as if some clairvoyant had just uttered future truth over him. Even though his heart was hurting at the time, he somehow believed that what Mama Maggie had said would happen.

He and Maria eventually did get back together. Maggie came to their wedding in the United States. When their first child, Alexander, was born, Mama Maggie held him in her arms, smiling.

MAMA MAGGIE IS NO JESUS. BUT THE FACT IS, SOME PEOPLE on this earth are *like* him—loving, giving, sacrificial. Many people she interacts with say that she is one of them.

Mama Maggie is fully present in this world. She's connected; if you're there to see her, then she is there to see you—except if you're in the slum, then the poor children always take priority. She loses herself in the kids. She cleans up children's messes; and hugs diseased people whom many would avoid.

She is practical and pretty relentless. She makes business plans with her staff and reviews her organization's statistics. She asks the hard questions. She laughs with her staff and her friends. As her niece Maria says, she can sit and chat with her like a girlfriend about clothes, ideas, news, whatever. She is fun and has great freedom. She does not judge. She tells people who get hung up on snarky details to chill out. She is not preoccupied but present. People want to be with her. She does not judge, spout out truisms, or look for the spotlight.

She's also a person who connects with God in an unusual way. Sometimes she is decidedly not present. She often removes herself. Much of her free time is spent in meditation, repentance, and reading of the Bible. She submits to ancient biblical disciplines. She fasts, denying herself normal physical needs. She will pray in a closet while the family goes on fun outings. She is in love with a power many cannot see.

She would be the first to say that unlike Jesus, she is quite flawed. But that's the beauty of her faith. People say that what is intriguing, alluring, and magnetic about Mama Maggie is the same thing that drew people to Jesus Christ two thousand years ago.

Love.

Chapter 24

Mama Maggie in Action: *Stop!*

To love means loving the unlovable. To forgive means pardoning
the unpardonable. Faith means believing the unbelievable.
Hope means hoping when everything seems hopeless.

—G. K. Chesterton

MAMA MAGGIE'S NEPHEW, BOSH GOBRAN, IS A THOUGHT-ful, funny man in his thirties. He founded NetEgypt, an Internet and mobile services company headquartered in Cairo. He loves his work, in part due to his clients who appreciate how much his company helps them succeed. And like many in the extended family, Mama Maggie's example has had a big impact on Bosh. He shares his aunt's compassion for the poor and uses his free time to do all kinds of charitable work for the garbage kids of Cairo.

For example, during the recent unusually harsh winter in Cairo, with its first snowfall in decades, Bosh knew that the poor were not prepared for the cold. The kids in the slums were freezing at night, burrowing into piles of trash in a vain attempt to get warm.

Inspired by Mama Maggie's maverick style, Bosh and his wife, Nada, with the help of his sister Nano Gobran, didn't wait for some other organization to help. They felt compelled to follow her "right now" example. They went to various stores and bought every blanket they could find. They bought every pullover sweater in stock. They talked to friends about the need, and as people in the affluent Heliopolis suburb chatted at their clubs, or corporate meetings, or at restaurants, and their talk inevitably turned to the harsh winter, they also thought about the poor in the slums. Because of Bosh and Nada's initiative, they now knew of a way to help those who were suffering. Their hearts were warmed. They gave money, Egyptians helping other Egyptians. A small tsunami of kindness ensued, and ultimately, tens of thousands of blankets and 9,800 pullover sweaters were given out to the garbage families in Cairo.

Bosh has had many appreciative customers in his years of building up his successful firm. That is a good thing. But Bosh says that serving the poor brought a better kind of satisfaction. He gave a blanket to a ragged, shivering woman. "*Rubina khaleek,*" she said in gratitude. "May our God keep you."

Her gratitude spurred Bosh on in a way that corporate success and kudos from clients can't quite match. It was stimulating to perceive a need and jump in to meet it. Mama Maggie's example of doing just that had primed him to respond, which made him hungry to respond again, whatever comes up.

Mama Maggie sees life differently from most of us, Bosh says. Many of us speed up, get stressed, and sometimes snappish, if we have too much to do. When we're very busy, says Bosh, "it's hard to sit. It's hard to really *see*."

Now, even as a busy man and successful globetrotter, he's learned to stop. To wait. And, like Mama Maggie, to think on a different plane, as much as he can.

MAMA MAGGIE SHARES HER PHILOSOPHIES WITH TWO writers from rather different traditions: Francis of Assisi and U.S. pastor Rick Warren. Saint Francis is one of Maggie's heroes. He said, in the thirteenth century, among many other things, "We should seek not so much to pray but to become prayer."

Rick Warren, pretty firmly established in the twenty-first century, wrote one of Mama Maggie's favorite books, *The Purpose Driven Life*, which has sold more than 30 million copies. The book resonated with principles Mama Maggie has held for years. She also loves a quote from his small book, *The Purpose of Christmas*. In it, among many other things, Warren writes, "The more you pray, the less you'll panic."

It's illogical in human terms: when she is busiest, or facing big opposition or an "impossible" project, Mama Maggie doesn't spin her wheels faster, stay up later, or try harder. She listens, meditates, and *stops*, thinking of what God would want.

During a recent staff meeting, Mama Maggie spoke to a group of about sixty female workers. They were mostly young women in their early twenties, excited about a two-day retreat in which they could connect with Mama Maggie and each other, and be inspired in their hard work.

As with every big staff gathering, the time started with everyone in the group standing and reading or reciting from memory a passage from the book of Matthew where Jesus lays out radical directives about life priorities and caring for the poor. The passage begins with the familiar words:

> *Blessed are the poor in spirit,*
> *for theirs is the kingdom of heaven.*
> *Blessed are those who mourn,*
> *for they will be comforted.*
> *Blessed are the meek,*
> *for they will inherit the earth.*

Blessed are those who hunger and thirst for righteousness,
for they will be filled.
Blessed are the merciful,
for they will be shown mercy.
Blessed are the pure in heart,
for they will see God.
Blessed are the peacemakers,
for they will be called children of God.
Blessed are those who are persecuted because of righteousness,
for theirs is the kingdom of heaven.[1]

The meeting went on, with guitars and enthusiastic singing. Leaders went up and down the rows of women, collecting written questions for Mama Maggie.

As Mama Maggie arrived, a young woman presented her with a huge sheaf of fresh flowers. Smiling, Mama Maggie began to methodically take the big bouquet apart, a move that seemed odd until she went up and down the aisles, passing individual flowers to every girl in the room.

Meanwhile, these young women pulled out very small notebooks and very sharp pencils and prepared to think.

A young woman at the front began writing some of the questions on a big white board.

The first two queries were unusual.

"How can I really change my bad habits?"

"What is spiritual ignorance?"

Mama Maggie began to address these by setting some basic foundations.

"Be sure that since you have joined the service of God's family, you are protected by him. Please feel happy. If you feel troubled or exhausted, you are not alone. You are within a group, and the whole group is protected. You are surrounded with love, if you were to feel this, you would know it is big grace. You are not alone whatever you pass through.

"Each one of us has a sort of revolution in our lives, and we write down bad things that we need to get rid of," said Mama Maggie. "If you have written down your faults, you've done the most difficult part, you've achieved 50 percent of the goal. When a problem comes out to the light, it will soon be resolved. So you've gone halfway by acknowledging this."

Mama Maggie acknowledged that changing, getting rid of weaknesses, is very hard. People can't do it on their own, she said. They need heavenly power to transform from the inside out.

"I can see God in each one of you," Mama Maggie continued. "That's why I love each one of you, because you are a beautiful creation by God. I love you, because I look at God and I see you in him, not because of what you do, but because of who you are in him.

"We don't know how long we will see each other. Like when the [Egyptian] revolution happened and the streets were dangerous, we didn't know if we would see each other again. If this is the last time I see you, I want to kiss each one of you, your hands and your feet, even if I couldn't tell this to you one hundred times, I want you to know there is someone on earth who loves you very much."

A girl raised her hand. "There are people where you feel how much they love God, they have a right heart. How do you get that way?"

"I was personally treated much better than I deserve by God," Mama Maggie said. "So I forgive others and love them like I've been loved. We belong to this world of human beings who received sin from Adam and Eve. The price of sin is death and so this is what we had deserved, but by the grace of God when Jesus came, was crucified on a cross, and rose from the dead, he delivered me from sin. We became the children of the King."

She went on, saying that ignoring spiritual realities takes human beings down to the level of a cat or dog, just focusing on what to eat or drink. Focusing only on material things robs human beings of what is truly of worth; you might gain the whole world, but lose your own soul.

This led to the next question, the one about spiritual ignorance.

"The opposite of the spiritually intelligent person," Mama Maggie responded, "is the person who can't feel God, because she is always busy doing something else, always distracted. It's like if you try to look at your reflection in water, you can't see yourself if the water is moving. You can only see yourself if the water is calm.

"Your body has to be still for your spirit to calm down. If you are running, you can't see clearly. Stopping and seeing, being still, is a gift from heaven.

"Today, in fact, God will give us this present of stillness," Mama Maggie continued, but no one in the room yet knew what she meant. She went on, "There is someone who said if you want to find the godly person, you will know him or her by his stillness. It is good to practice silence in front of God. This is the school of grace.

"Sometimes I'm controlling my mouth, but maybe my mind is racing. We have to learn how to quiet our minds."

Mama Maggie likened it to a small child learning to walk. At first, she or he falls down all the time. But gradually, the child learns how to stay upright and walk. It's the same with the discipline of silence and focus on spiritual realities. In the beginning, we all are horribly distracted. *Hmm, what about that e-mail? Did I call Michael back? What about that report, that deadline, that assignment? Should I change my job? How about my hair color?*

But eventually, Mama Maggie reminded the women, with practice, we all can learn to stop. To be silent, not just in our bodies, but in our restless minds.

"Sometimes we are very busy, we pass on all the things that are making us sad. Real life is not about having money, because money will not satisfy the deepest part of ourselves. We can use it, but we shouldn't let money use us. If God gives it to me, I use it according to his will. I can't love material things. I can like the way a chair or anything else looks, but not love it. Things cannot be my god.

"Even if people think you are good," Mama Maggie continued, "this is not important. It is important what *God* thinks of you. Don't talk a lot about earthly things. God can give you peace and quietness right in the midst of chaos or troubles. He can meet our needs.

"And all that's happening in our country, the struggles of any country, God is in control. There is a new heaven and a new earth coming, where God will live with human beings."

Mama Maggie went on to say that thinking about that future to come gives her the ability to overcome habits of trying to control things or thinking too much about herself. "Every good thing is from God's grace, every talent, good feeling: all from God.

"I know that God has started something good in every one of us. I ask that God would make his grace bigger in all of us. We can have a new start every day, every hour. He can make all things new as we trust in him.

"We will do this today.

"When a child has a new toy, she is distracted by it and forgets her mother. Some of us have gotten distracted and forgotten our Father. If your phone rings, and you feel that you *have* to answer it, you are its slave."

As Mama Maggie continued, it became apparent to the staff

women that something unusual was about to take place. She proceeded to tell them they were taking a twenty-four-hour break . . . a break from talking. This is very hard for twenty-somethings, regardless of culture. The young women loved Mama Maggie, but there were murmurs. Some of the women in the room were accepting, some resigned but willing. Others were worried.

"What if my family needs to get in touch with me?" one asked. "What about my brother who is sick? What about the work to be done?"

Mama Maggie was smiling and tender, yet firm, a straight arrow of a person in her humble white clothing, dark socks, brown sandals, and a determined demeanor. "If you set time to spend with God, he will take care of everything else. Will the whole ministry fall down? Might human silence bring about *God's* failure?

"This is not my ministry," she said. "This is *God's* ministry. He will take care of it.

"We start now, two o'clock, until two o'clock tomorrow afternoon. It's going to be a time of total silence," said Mama Maggie.

A leader, only slightly less surprised than the girls, came through the room with a big plastic bag, collecting everyone's cell phones.

"Forget everything at home," Mama Maggie continued. "How many of you think that today is not a good time for silence and repentance?"

No hands went up.

"I am glad that none of you feels this way. Don't be afraid. God will lead you."

Mama Maggie left the training room. Including herself in the twenty-four-hour season of silence, she walked wordlessly through the grounds, checking new plants and picking up a stone or two to tuck in her pocket. Then she silently waved and climbed into the battered ministry vehicle that would take her home.

This counterintuitive power of quiet is central to what Mama Maggie is doing in the slums of the Middle East. She's not just instilling work skills but a mind-set that undergirds the work in the next generation of compassionate people who go to the slums. She really believes that strength comes through stillness and focus on the Light, that God infuses people with his power if they depend on him. She has seen this in the characters of biblical days—improbable, flawed people doing the same. She is living it out in twenty-first-century Egypt, in a very politically complicated place.

She is not just a power-of-positive-thinking do-gooder, wonderful as that is. She is seeking to go to the core of the nature of human beings. For Mama Maggie, the work of touching lives has to do with not just helping human bodies but nourishing human souls.

In other settings, many business meetings focus on *what* staff members are doing. Mama Maggie focuses on *who* staff people are . . . their character and how they are drawing on spiritual resources within to really give something of permanence to the poor.

So Mama Maggie's leadership of her team is not all about techniques for distribution of services, as important as it is to deliver help in an efficient way. It is about relationships with God and each other. It's about a pervasive higher power that can run through the human spirit, connecting people to one another, and in turn giving impoverished families hope. It is about equipping slum children to dream new dreams, dreams that are bigger than a piece of tomato or a bed.

—— Chapter 25 ——

Small Girls, Big Dreams

I have for many years endeavored to make this vital truth clear; and
still people marvel when I tell them that I am happy. They imagine
that my limitations weigh heavily upon my spirit, and chain me to
the rock of despair. Yet, it seems to me, happiness has very little
to do with the senses. If we make up our minds that this is a drab
and purposeless universe, it will be that, and nothing else. On the
other hand, if we believe that the earth is ours, and that the sun and
moon hang in the sky for our delight, there will be joy upon the hills
and gladness in the fields because the Artist in our souls glorifies
creation. Surely, it gives dignity to life to believe that we are born
into this world for noble ends, and that we have a higher destiny than
can be accomplished within the narrow limits of this physical life.

—Helen Keller

MAMA MAGGIE TEACHES PEOPLE TO DREAM, AND THAT'S clear in an outpost, one of the smaller projects of her work in Egypt. Though it is not in the business of running orphanages, the ministry has two group homes in Cairo for boys and girls who have nowhere else to go.

The children are not all technically orphans. Some have fathers who abandoned the family by leaving after the mother died or who have chemical addictions that have caused them to neglect their children. Egypt's government outlaws adoption, so the best option for these children is to live in a secure setting where they have food, clothing, shelter, education, spiritual instruction, and a "family" of Stephen's Children workers who care for them.

This small home in a decent Cairo neighborhood is refuge to giggly, shy girls who are ready to tell you their hopes for the future if you just ask. They don't want to talk about their pasts.

There are two sisters: their mother burned to death, and their dad married again and forgot his first family. Another girl is from a family of seven girls. Her father beat her. Another girl's mom was in an accident and was half-paralyzed. Her father forced the young children to work, took their money, and spent it on alcohol. Another was the only girl in a home with six brothers. She had a baby sister, but the infant died after a rat chewed on her head. Her mother is mentally incompetent; her father chose to feed the family donkey rather than the children.

The stories of the past could go on and on.

One evening the older girls prepare chicken livers and rice in the kitchen, and the younger girls set the table for dinner. These girls are all in school; time for homework is a priority in the big daily schedule that is posted on the wall.

One teenaged girl wants to be an accountant. A sunny, small girl, wearing a cartoon dog on her pink shirt, says she wants to "serve in the church." A slender teenager with a patient face says she wants to be a doctor. With prompting from her leaders, she goes to another room and gets a drawing she did some time ago. It is the crayoned picture of a beautiful home with three stories. It sits on a beach. The sun is shining; the water is clear, deep blue. There is a garden and a cat. "When I am a doctor," she says, "I will have an orphanage like this. The first floor is for babies. The second is for children. And the third is for old people."

The youngest girl in the room, a smiley girl wearing a pink velour shirt, blurts out at high volume, "Wait! I didn't get to say my dream yet! I want to be one of the servants with Mama Maggie!"

Youssef notes that this little orphanage only houses this small group of girls. It's not a huge enterprise, a conveyer belt of impressive statistics saving the world. Such things don't really exist. He tells the familiar story of the starfish.

A man was walking along a beach after a high tide. Hundreds of starfish had washed up on the shore. The man saw a young boy who was walking the beach. He would bend over, pick up a dying starfish, and fling it back into the life-giving waters. Then he'd go a few yards, pick up the next, and do the same.

"What are you doing?" the man yelled at the boy. "There are thousands of starfish on this beach. Nothing you can do can possibly make a difference."

The boy held out the starfish he had just picked up, then threw it into the ocean. "It makes a difference to that one," he said.

The beautiful "starfish" who've been rescued and live in the Stephen's Children girls' orphanage know they are part of a family, even during the volatile history in Cairo over the past few years, when there have been times of chaos on the streets.

During one such period, when there were unruly demonstrations and turmoil, Cairo's police were unreliable. Lawless elements took advantage of the lack of security and general chaos to loot businesses and rob homes. Neighbors had to band together to protect their property.

In Youssef's neighborhood, the men divided into shifts and took turns defending their apartment building. They were armed with baseball bats and thick sticks. Youssef says the atmosphere, while tense, was actually also festive. People made popcorn to share; others brought juice and cookies or cakes down to the street. He got to know some of his neighbors—Muslims and Christians alike—whom he hadn't met before, as they all stood together to guard their homes.

Youssef happens to live around the corner from the girls' orphanage. On the first night of chaos in the streets, he got a call from one of the Stephen's Children female workers there.

"Oh, Mr. Youssef!" she quavered. "There are all these people yelling in the streets, and we are so frightened! Can you come?"

"You stay with me on the phone," Youssef responded. "Don't hang up. I'll be there as soon as I can."

She didn't know that Youssef lives less than a block away. He grabbed one of his neighbors, and within about thirty seconds, he told the worker to look out the front window of the orphanage. "Do you see me?" he asked, waving. "See, my friend and I are right here. We will take care of you!"

"Oh, Mr. Youssef!" she responded. "How in the world did you do that? Now I can breathe again!"

"You would have thought she was seeing King Kong out there in the street for her," Youssef says. "It was just me. But we stick together."

— *Chapter 26* —

Flames and Forgiveness

*The unity between Muslims and Coptic Christians
of Egypt is something of absolute importance.*

—H.E. Professor Dr. Sheikh Ahmad Muhammad
Al-Tayyeb, Grand Sheikh of Al-Azhar University,
Grand Imam of the Al-Azhar Mosque

*If you burn the churches, we will pray with our brothers in
the mosques, and if you burn the mosques, Muslims will pray
with us in the church, and if you burn them both, we're all
going to pray together in the streets, protecting each other.*

—The Coptic Orthodox Pope, His Holiness Tawadros II

꩜

No story set in Egypt would be complete without trying to tell a bit of its complex historical context, which of course affects Mama Maggie and her work, though she takes no sides in political matters. She loves Egypt.

In the summer of 2013, Egypt was home to the biggest political demonstration in human history. Helicopters circled Cairo, rotor blades beating, engines throbbing, their crews peering down on millions of human beings thronging the streets. The people filled the downtown squares, overflowing to the bridges crossing the Nile River, clogging the curbs in front of the presidential palace, spilling over into alleys and side streets everywhere.

From above, the people looked like a huge mass of ants. The feeling on the ground was more personal. There were signs, banners, and Egyptian flags; the streets thundered with the sounds of voices, millions strong, singing patriotic songs, shouting for change. Ordinary people who had never marched in a political protest in their lives had come to the streets. Thirty million of them. They had packed bags of food and drink; some had chosen to wear comfortable shoes, just in case events turned violent and they needed to run. They came with their friends, neighbors, and families. They bought roasted corn and colorful hats from sidewalk vendors. Many had brought red cards, the international soccer symbol used to ban a player from the field: it was time to ban Egypt's then-president from the fields of power.

According to the demonstration's organizers, 22 million Egyptians had signed a petition demanding that their president, Mohammed Morsi, step down. Many felt that the Muslim Brotherhood, which he represented, had no real interest in Egypt, per se, other than spreading Islamist ideals throughout the Middle East. "The demonstrations . . . reflect the growing polarization of the nation since Morsi took power, with the president and his Islamist allies in one camp and seculars, liberals, moderate Muslims and Christians on the other," one outlet reported.[1]

Twelve months earlier, Egyptians had hoped that Mohammed Morsi might escort them out of the autocratic rule of former president Hosni Mubarak. After thirty years in power, Mubarak had been ousted in the gripping events of the Arab Spring in 2011. After his fall, and after close and contested elections, Morsi had taken the helm of Egypt. (Many Egyptians tell the joke of a man who votes in an election. He changes his mind and comes back the next day. "I need to change my vote," he says. "Don't worry," officials tell him. "We already did that for you.")

"Mr. Morsi entered office on a wave of hope," writer Alaa Al Aswany editorialized in the *New York Times*. "In June 2012, millions streamed onto the streets to celebrate his victory, but their elation soon turned into hopelessness and then rage as they discovered that he was a puppet controlled by the [Muslim] Brotherhood's supreme leader. That November, Mr. Morsi issued a decree annulling the Constitution and granting himself sweeping powers over the legal system."[2]

By summer 2013, a year into President Morsi's term, Egypt's economy was in distress. Power blackouts were daily events. The national debt was growing, as devaluation crippled the Egyptian currency. The government banned the iconic opera *Aida* for being too secular. Many Egyptians believed that Morsi and the Muslim Brotherhood leaders were ruining the country, focusing more on operationalizing Islam into policy, both domestic and regional, rather than focusing on the best interests of the Egyptian people.

The people's decision to march in the streets had been deliberate, serious, perhaps life-altering, but now the atmosphere on the street was like a party. Muslims, Christians, everyone stood together, eating popcorn and looking for a new beginning in Egypt. Many had never engaged in any sort of political activity, like a small, determined woman we'll call Nerim. She took up a position near the presidential palace. She had never marched in a protest in her life. In her daily routines, she just obeyed the law, dealt with chaos on the streets as it affected her, and kept a low profile, like the rest of her extended family.

But with the excesses of the current regime, it was time to go to the streets. When they had discussed it as a group, the male members of Nerim's family said that just the men would come out to protest. The streets might be dangerous. All of perhaps ninety pounds, Nerim said no. "No. We will march together for freedom," she informed everyone. "We will stand together as a family."

Nerim and her family came to the street each day for four days to protest. They saw army helicopters circling overhead. The crowd cheered for them; the helicopter crews dropped thousands of tiny Egyptian flags, their red fabric flapping in the breeze.

An elderly woman near Nerim had never been in a protest before either. She wasn't quite sure what to do. But, she told Nerim, in a simple way, "We are coming to say no to Morsi . . . We had Mubarak for thirty years. He was bad, but he was one of us. This guy, Morsi, is not one of us."

Other older Egyptians, part of a class that had prospered for many years, were not content to sit home and be comfortable. Elderly doctors, lawyers, engineers, accountants: they marched in the streets as well. It was time for a change. Egypt needed a new beginning, and her people were pleading for it. Mama Maggie herself had draped a large Egyptian flag outside her apartment and had gone to a monastery in Upper Egypt to fast and pray for her country.

One man we'll call Alexander watched as the flags fluttered down from the helicopters circling above the crowd. His wife, at home with their two young children, had been worried about his safety when he said he wanted to come to the protest, but he had told her he *had* to march in the streets.

"I don't want to be part of the 'Couch Party,'" he had said, referring to those who were waiting out the demonstrations on TV at home on their sofas.

"Okay," his wife had responded. "You go. I will pray!"

Later, in his sector of the enormous crowd, Alexander saw a teenager climb up on his friends' backs to write on a street sign. The people nearby cheered and waited as he steadied himself and pulled out his marker, ready to scrawl a few words for freedom.

The boy hesitated, started to write, then stopped. It soon became apparent to those who were watching that he actually did not know how to post his slogan.

An elderly woman in the crowd saw his dilemma. She was good-natured but blunt: "You see," she yelled, "*this* is why we need a new government. We have eighteen-year-olds whose education is so poor that they do not even know how to write!"

Over the next few days of demonstrations, the whole world watched as Egypt swayed. By July 4, the army responded to the masses and, with warning, removed Mr. Morsi from office, with General Abdel Fattah el-Sisi, commander in chief of the Egyptian Armed Forces, informing him he was no longer president. An interim president and government were established until the Constitution could be rewritten and new elections could be held. Critics noted that during Morsi's administration, he had ignored key issues, done little to alleviate the continued wreckage of Egypt's economy, and instead spent valuable parliamentary time on such things as trying to institute a law lowering the legal age of marriage for girls to nine years old.[3]

Morsi's removal was controversial. It was condemned by the United States and other governments around the world. Many in the West called it a coup. But the Egyptian people who had gone to the streets really didn't see it that way. They believed the deposition of Morsi to be the imposition of a pluralistic majority removing a dangerous leader.

"We believed our president had violated the will of the people," said one marcher. "We have no impeachment process. He was killing Egypt. Whether you are Muslim or Christian, we love Egypt. And if Morsi had stayed in power through the rest of his term, there would be no more Egypt."

Various Egyptian leaders stood with General el-Sisi as he announced on television that Morsi was gone. One was the Coptic pope, Tawadros II. Another was the grand imam of Al-Azhar, Ahmad Al-Tayyeb, considered one of the world's most preeminent Muslim leaders.

What would el-Sisi, eventually elected president of the country in 2014, bring to Egypt? At that time, no one knew. Some feared a return to restrictive, army control of the nation. But the vast majority saw him as a savior. Egypt has important economic and geopolitical problems ahead. It remains to be seen what will happen there. But back in the days when Mr. Morsi fell, events took place that caught the attention of the world.

According to various media, Muslim Brotherhood members were furious that the Coptic pope had stood with el-Sisi on television.

"The pope . . . is involved in the removal of the first elected Islamist president," fumed writers on the Facebook page of the Brotherhood's Freedom and Justice Party. Others fomented violent reprisals against Christians. This, in spite of the fact that raw numbers showed that "far more Muslims opposed Morsi than Christians."[4]

Meanwhile, Mr. Morsi was imprisoned to wait for trial, along with dozens of codefendants, on charges of conspiring with foreign groups to destabilize Egypt, as well as inciting people to "commit crimes of deliberate and premeditated murder" and encouraging the "use of violence, thuggery, coercion, possession of firearms, ammunition and melee weapons, and unlawfully arresting, detaining, and torturing peaceful demonstrators."[5]

Morsi's supporters took to the streets. They filled Tahrir Square, Cairo's best-known site for demonstrations, squatting in makeshift tents, using the streets as toilets, blaring pro-Morsi speeches from loudspeakers. Government tanks and troops established positions around the square. Counterprotestors threw rocks. The new government imposed a curfew as all of Egypt simmered with barely contained mass violence.

On the evening of August 6, 2013, a Coptic girl, ten-year-old Jessica Boulous, was walking home from Bible class in Cairo with her teacher. The woman turned to buy something from a stall in an outdoor market. There was a single shot. The teacher swirled around to find little Jessica lying in a pool of blood. The Muslim shopkeeper rushed out, covered Jessica with his shirt, and took her to the hospital, but the bullet had gone through her heart. She was already dead.

No one claimed responsibility for the killing.[6]

Egyptian television broadcast a report showing radical Islamists attacking a police station in the town of Kerdasa on August 14 with rocket-propelled grenades, causing the deaths of fifteen policemen. They stripped the bodies and paraded them on the street.

On August 15, government security forces raided the entrenched camps in Cairo, forcibly moving protesters out. Tragically, many Morsi supporters were killed.

Almost immediately, churches across Egypt began to burn.

In the Church of the Virgin Mary in Al Nazla, a small village a few hours outside of Cairo, a large crowd burst through its gates, shouting slogans against Christians and calling for Egypt to become an Islamic state. Once they had looted the church, members of the crowd lobbed Molotov cocktails into it until the four-hundred-year-old structure was completely consumed in flames.[7]

St. George Church in Sontag, south of Cairo: stormed and burned.

Prince Tadros Church in Fayoum, southwest of Cairo: destroyed.

Various Catholic churches and monasteries were torched. The principal of a Catholic school in Bani Suef had assumed her school would be safe, as it educated equal numbers of Christians and Muslims. Not so. A mob broke into the school, stole computers and furniture, and set the building on fire. They knocked the cross off the street gate and replaced it with a black Islamist banner similar to the al-Qaida flag. They dragged the principal and two other nuns outside, parading them through the streets until a former teacher at the school, a Muslim, rescued them.[8]

In various villages in Upper Egypt, Christian-owned businesses had already been marked with an ominous black X. Now they burned.

In Minya, a mob attacked and destroyed a Coptic Christian orphanage, leaving two hundred children terrified and without shelter.

The Egyptian Bible Society has been quietly selling Bibles, books, and children's materials for a hundred years in Egypt. At its bookshops in Minya and Assiut, attackers demolished the metal doors, broke the windows, and set them on fire, reducing all the books and Bibles to ash.

In Kerdasa, just outside Cairo, where policemen had been attacked and killed, a mob broke down the gate of a Coptic church complex. They stole anything that could be carried, then set the rest on fire with Molotov cocktails and gasoline. One of the attackers left scrawled graffiti that read: "Egypt is Islamic."[9]

One of Mama Maggie's kindergartens was burned, but not before the perpetrators looted its computers and the other supplies that served the 270 poor children who attended it. (Afterward, one little boy brought a makeshift piggy bank to Mama Maggie, wanting to help fund the reconstruction of his school. Donors from Egypt rallied together and gave the money needed to rebuild the kindergarten.)

The attacks, in dozens of locations, were conducted in a uniform way, with looting, burning, and destruction. Christians in Egypt had been an often-persecuted minority for years, but violence on this scale had not been seen since the Middle Ages. Approximately 160 historic churches, businesses, homes, and cars owned by Christians were destroyed.

Many blamed extremists of the Muslim Brotherhood for the attacks, noting that ordinary Muslims had tried to help to defend the churches. Muslims and Christians live without question together, and have for generations. They look out for each other. But sometimes terrorists and troublemakers come.

Many news reports picked up interviews and images of Muslims trying to protect their Christian neighbors. One young man from Assiut expressed both concern and disgust at the actions by extremists.

"These people [attacking churches and Copts] are not Muslim, and they do not know what Islam is."[10]

In some places, Muslim men made a protective circle around Christian churches, protecting those inside. Christians had done the same, protecting Muslims who were praying, during chaotic political events in the Arab Spring of 2011.

Regardless of the perpetrators and their motivations, something remarkable happened in the smoldering ashes of Egypt's burned churches. In one town after another, banners were raised over the ruined buildings. Charred walls were scrawled with messages for the attackers.

The messages?

"We forgive!" "We still love you!" And on the burned wall of the ruined orphanage: "You meant to hurt us, but we forgive you. God is love. Everything works out for good."

A *60 Minutes* news crew visited the church in Kerdasa just after it had been burned. Services were being held in the only corner of the church that had not been totally destroyed.

"We were surprised," said veteran CBS journalist Bob Simon, "there was no anger, no call for revenge." As one of the senior clerics from the church told Simon, "Forgiveness is a very important principle in the Christian life."[11]

This overall response—from church after church after church—of grace and pardon from Egypt's Christians was not wasted on thoughtful Muslim observers. One of Mama Maggie's friends, a Christian, was talking with one of his Muslim friends at work. The colleague was talking about the outbreaks of violence, the burnings, and the banners that had cropped up on the ruined churches.

"As a Muslim, I knew Christianity had to do with forgiveness," he said. "But I never knew it would go to this extent."

Chapter 27

Simple Work, with Great Love

Miracles are a retelling in small letters of the very same story which is written across the whole world in letters too large for some of us to see.

—C. S. Lewis

⁊⊙⊙⊱

I N   T H E   A F T E R M A T H   O F   T H E   C H U R C H   B U R N I N G S ,   A N
Egyptian pastor mused that in spite of the pain, perhaps all this
really could be used for good. He happens to be a Protestant, but the
burnings affected Copts, Catholics, Anglicans, and Protestants with
equal-opportunity hatred.

"For years our buildings have been the center of our lives," this
man said, noting all the great meals, meetings, and conferences held
at the beautiful churches. "We were always there, together, behind
the walls of the church. Now the walls have been burned down.
Maybe God is telling us to go out, out to the communities, to help
people in need."

In spite of the various hassles, troubles, and violence that affect
their daily lives, the Christians of Egypt are not hopeless victims.
They have guts and courage in stormy times. As Father Anthony
Messeh, a popular Coptic priest in the Washington, DC, area, has
put it, "Where it is windy, trees' roots grow deeper. That is true of
the Christians in Egypt as well. Their stories are full of hope, resilience, love and forgiveness . . . even as attacks against them have
continued."

In the midst of the burning and looting, another threat loomed large: kidnapping.

According to Ezzat Ibrahim, director of the World Center for Human Rights in Minya and Asyut, "In the year 2013, 69 Christians were abducted in Minya governorate. Four of them were killed because their families were unable to pay the kidnappers that demanded ransoms, four of them were returned by the police, and 61 Christians were returned after their families paid a ransom from fifty thousand Egyptians pounds ($7,000) to several million Egyptian pounds."[1]

A middle-aged Christian doctor in Minya was kidnapped and tortured until his wife paid a large ransom. He had been thrown into a pit, a gun held against his ear, then his forehead, his mouth; he was sure he was going to die.

"I never thought I could take one millionth of what I endured," he says. "But every step of the way, every moment of pain, I could feel God there with me."[2]

One of Mama Maggie's male staff workers in a dangerous area of Egypt kissed his kindergarten-aged son good-bye one morning after breakfast, and the little boy headed off to walk to school as usual. Later, when the father left home, he found his son's shoes in the street. He picked them up and took them to the school . . . where he discovered that his son had never arrived for kindergarten.

The little boy had been kidnapped. The police were of no help. Then the ransom demand came.

Everyone at Stephen's Children prayed and rallied around the frightened family. In the end, the ransom was paid. The child returned home.

In Mokattam, a teenaged boy named Essam was kidnapped from near one of Mama Maggie's kindergartens. A group of masked men asked him if he was a Christian. "Yes," he said. They cut him with knives, tied his feet to the back of their car, dragged him, then put him in a body bag and jumped on him. They left him for dead.

Miraculously, he survived.

The *Christian Science Monitor* reports that Christians are targeted for kidnapping because "they do not have tribes or families who retaliate, unlike many Muslims in southern Egypt. As a tight-knit minority community, they are also perceived as able to raise large sums of money from friends and relatives for ransom."[3]

The chief of the African and Middle Eastern Division of the Library of Congress says that the Copts are "an easy target" for those who want to stir up chaos and violence. But, she points out, in spite of hardship, threats, and violence, "they see their history going back to ancient times. Over the millennium, they've been attacked and survived. They see their destiny as being rooted in Egypt."[4]

Rooted in Egypt.

In spite of the pressures, hassles, and dangers they face every day, Mama Maggie's team in Egypt has chosen to stay in Egypt in a time when many Egyptians have chosen to emigrate. They serve thirty thousand poor families every day. They love their country, though there is no question that those who chose to leave love their country as well. They love their Muslim neighbors and friends, and, extraordinarily, as in the cases of the church burnings and so much more, they love their enemies, the few extremists who seem to have chosen to wage war on so many.

"Difficulties strengthen us," one man said. "We prefer to die in Egypt, not ask for help from abroad. Our eyes are on God. Just let people know the situation in Egypt."

One man who had been helped by Stephen's Children said that his house was surrounded one dark night by a mob of men with long knives. They were chanting, yelling, taunting him to come out so they could kill him.

The man stepped out. He focused on just one young man in the mob. "Why do you hate me?" he asked.

The would-be assailant could not answer.

The Christian man looked him in the eye. "I don't hate you," he said. "I love you."

The crowd of people slowly melted away in the dark.

Mama Maggie loves her homeland. She loves her Muslim friends, neighbors, and all the families and children her ministry serves, regardless of their religion. She prays constantly for the good of her nation, for whatever government that is in place there. She grieves for Egyptians of every background who are threatened, bereaved, and in pain of all kinds. Meanwhile, she plans new initiatives, visits small children in the slums, and retreats to the desert to pray, during which times her large team of workers feel a mysterious infusion of energy and encouragement.

So, in her paradoxical, mystical, practical way, Mama Maggie presses on. The focus of her story is never on the challenges that may exist around her, tough as they are. The focus is on the children and the families—Muslims and Christians alike—who need the powerful touch of love and hope in the slums. During the recent years of violence and political turmoil, Mama Maggie has had many invitations to leave Egypt, for her own safety.

"Jesus would not leave," she says. "He would stay with his people. I must do the same."

In the context of Egypt today—vibrant, volatile, occasionally violent—Mama Maggie says, with characteristic vision, "I want to go on with our work for the poor more and more, until it spreads all over Egypt, the Middle East, and the whole world, to make a better future for humanity—especially the children.

"This is the *real* love story, the one that lasts forever," she continues. "How many love stories on earth end or change within just a few years? As we set our minds on God, who loved us, and gave himself for us, we are filled up. In the poor areas, we provide simple work, but with great love. We draw a smile in the heart and spirit of every deprived child. I hope this goes on from generation to generation to generation."

A Note from Marty
Makary: Beginnings

THE MORNING SUN LIT THE CITY OF CAIRO AS I PEERED
through the window of my hotel room. In the distance I saw what
many describe as the greatest of the seven wonders of the world—
the pyramids of Giza—rising improbably and perfectly out of the
sand. Architects still debate how these spectacles were built with such
remarkable precision more than four thousand years ago.

I had seen the pyramids before. But this morning they spoke
mightily and humbled me. I was in an extraordinary land—an ancient
ground with a modern society buzzing about.

It was time to go. I reluctantly turned away from the view to
double-check what was in my medical bag. I had come to Cairo
because I heard that an Egyptian relative, Maggie Gobran, needed
a doctor for the people she served in the city's slums.

I was born in England, grew up in Pennsylvania, and didn't yet
know Maggie well. But I had heard that something amazing was happening in her work among the poor. She was known locally as "Mama
Maggie," a name given her by the many children who saw her as
mother to them. A band of impressive local Egyptians came alongside
of her, and together, their story had been noticed by humanitarians

and people in positions of power around the world. At the time of my visit, however, I just knew vaguely that Mama Maggie was doing something good. I didn't know what to expect.

Smothered in cultural expressions of hospitality, logistical communications in Egypt can be difficult to decipher. My team and I had been given fragmented, third-hand instructions to meet a fellow named Youssef, who had worked with Mama Maggie for years, outside our hotel lobby at 9:00 a.m.

With our bags of medications, stethoscopes, and notepads, we stood at the hotel entrance, along a grand driveway. Doormen in crisp uniforms greeted diplomats, contractors, and distinguished visitors from around the world. A line of gleaming black Mercedes waited to transport people to important meetings throughout Cairo.

In the royal lineup of luxury cars there was a standout: a rickety Isuzu minivan nicked with dents and spotted with rust, its seats sagging. It puttered asthmatically at the curb. The driver, an energetic, green-eyed man with a giant smile, saw us. He jumped out of his battered vehicle, made his way toward us, and introduced himself.

"Welcome, welcome!" he shouted, grabbing our hands. "Welcome to Cairo!"

Youssef had arrived . . . and I knew today was going to be an adventure.

He packed us into the stuttering minivan. "Do you need coffee?" he asked. "Tea? How was your trip? How did you sleep? Please make yourselves comfortable!"

Instantly, it was as if we were best friends. We talked about our families and our countries. My colleagues and I looked out the car windows at an extraordinary metropolis, one of the oldest continuous civilizations on the planet.

Cairo was loud, hot, and wonderfully congested. Vendors strode through traffic selling sweets, balloons, packets of Kleenex, you name it. Cars, people, scooters, and the occasional donkey cart all paraded through the crowded streets.

Our ride became bumpier as the Isuzu—its poor shock absorbers long gone—jiggled through potholes in the pavement, where there actually was pavement. Soon we were on dirt roads at the outskirts of the city limits, with the sprawling complex of Cairo on one side, and on the other side, the seemingly endless sands of the Great Sahara desert.

Youssef navigated torturous dirt paths and huge piles of trash. Our trust in the Isuzu brand grew stronger as the small van rocked and pitched like a boat in stormy swells.

Out the window, the scene began to deteriorate. Towering, crumbling brick buildings with broken-out windows were covered with trash as far as I could see. The streets were narrow, grimy pathways, filled with bags of waste. Thin donkeys plodded by, their carts piled with loads of refuse. Barefoot children climbed on mountains of plastic bottles, rotting food, and sharp debris. They picked through the garbage competing with feral dogs and cats doing the same thing. The stench of rot and sewage was overwhelming.

"Ah!" said Youssef. "We are here."

He went on to tell us how this hellish place had come to exist years ago.

When life in the Egyptian countryside became too difficult because of economic troubles or religious persecution—sometimes both—the poorest rural Egyptians would flee to Cairo. Many were illiterate. Almost all were Christian, though many had never actually heard of Jesus. They could not afford to live in the capital city or its suburbs. Many would move to the garbage district with nothing except what they could carry. Their homes were originally tin huts made of barrels they found in the trash. Today there is a mixture of shanties and decaying urban apartments. The majority have no electricity, no clean water, and no sewage systems.

At our hotel, the Isuzu had been a shunned junk car. Here in the garbage village, next to the donkeys and other dubious forms of transportation, it was a marvelous and sophisticated vehicular machine. We pulled up to the gate of a complex located in the midst of the congested squalor and chaos. I climbed out and picked my way across trash in the dust.

Youssef led me through the door at the gate. Suddenly, I was in a different place. I saw a remarkably clean haven. It was a large, open courtyard, swept clean of trash. Crowds of kids were clustered with adults in various groups. One group had professional-looking men my age patiently teaching small children in ninety-five-degree temperatures. Others played soccer. A third group was singing. A fourth group of children was lined up to receive plates full of food.

It was a bit hard to get my bearings. The stench of the slum had created more than just a physical reaction in me. It was depressing, oppressive. But here, though we were still in the slum, I felt that the heavy feeling of despair had evaporated. As I was still realizing this, Youssef put me into a line of people edging, one by one, toward a bench, a basin, and a water pump. There were small children, covered with dust and dirt, waiting in line. And me.

I waited, watching what happened when the child in front of me had his turn. He sat on the bench and put his legs in the low basin. There was a lady dressed in white, sitting on the other end of the bench. She turned on the spigot. Clean water flowed in a stream all over the child's filthy feet. She rubbed his toes with soap, lathering him up to his knees. He laughed, and she did too.

Then she rinsed his feet and legs, put them in her own lap, covered by towels, and gently dried him off. I could barely hear what she whispered in his ear in Arabic: "I love you. I am proud of you. You are a good boy!"

Then she took a pair of new, clean sandals—in a place where most children have no shoes at all—and placed them on his feet. She kissed his feet tenderly, called him by name, and told him again that she loved him. He got up, a big smile on his face.

The idea of washing people's feet—and kissing them—was foreign to me. I had never experienced it, only heard of it as an ancient biblical practice of hospitality in desert lands. I remembered historically that Jesus had washed his friends' feet, surprising them because it was considered a lowly job.

At the front of the line, the woman in white was doing this very thing. I felt uncomfortable. I would have gotten out of line if I could have. But when my turn came, I slowly sat on the bench. I took off my dusty shoes, covered with the grime of the ghetto. I submitted myself to the ritual.

The woman in white was Mama Maggie. She smiled, but said nothing. She put my feet under the cool water. She lathered them with a bar of soap, rinsed them, and dried them in her lap. She gave me new shoes.

I felt undeserving, yet clean. No words. I kissed her on the cheek and got up. I was walking now on new ground.

I was led by a colleague of Mama Maggie's to a small medical clinic in the complex. I opened my doctor bag as about fifty children lined up to see me, holding hands and waiting patiently in perfect formation.

As I examined the children, I realized that my medical bag did not have what these kids needed. What they needed was someone to hug them, talk to them, and play with them, someone to give them the dignity of calling them by their name and to tell them that they were loved.

I was taken to a factory Mama Maggie had purchased and converted to a vocational training center so the kids would learn handiwork skills to get jobs. We went to a school where there was a big luncheon for kids, with long lines of children waiting patiently for chicken and rice they could never receive in their own homes. We went to a women's center where vibrant Egyptian women were teaching adult classes on hygiene and healthy family life to their sisters who were mostly illiterate, abused, and otherwise without hope.

Before I visited the garbage district, I had expected long faces of hopelessness among the residents. Instead, I was astonished by the unlikely characteristics of this community—encouragement, appreciation, smiles, giggles, and joy. Even though many of the children and moms had difficult lives, they kissed one another on both cheeks, welcomed visitors, hugged, and laughed . . . a lot. This was a happy place.

I saw that the staff and volunteers who worked with Mama Maggie were remarkably energized too, with a tangible sense of purpose. They seemed to have a special joy that came from helping those with real emotional wounds. It was good.

The paradoxical contentment of their work in the slum challenged me to think about what makes people happy.

I live in a pretty acquisitive culture, one that values owning things and individual gain over community gain. A higher income. A better look. More power at work. Membership in various circles. A bigger house. An unconscious tendency to measure people by their "net worth."

I found myself asking if my success was bringing the fulfillment I now observed among those serving the garbage kids.

As I watched the extraordinary work there in Cairo giving hope and smiles to families and loving kids who may have never experienced love, I wondered if I missing out on that joy in my daily life.

Perhaps the things that kept me busy were distractions from experiencing true happiness in the way these people were experiencing it.

Though these thoughts were quick, they later began to challenge me the next time I found myself using the words *need* and *worth*. I found that I was thinking a bit differently about routine life and the vocabulary that defines my norms. Fresh memories of the images of smiles and the sounds of cheering of the garbage kids were imprinted on my mind. Life back home now had a new context. My reflex to get frustrated with a taxi driver who went the long route seemed trivial, a futile expenditure of my emotion. My disappointment that the supermarket was closed when I arrived at 9:00 p.m. now seemed myopic. And my anger at the injustice of paying for hidden bank fees seemed inconsequential.

I was so moved by the genuine happiness I saw in Maggie and her staff from serving others that I invited my friend Ellen Vaughn to see what was happening in Egypt. I knew that Ellen loves to search out stories of what creative people are doing around the world to help others and discover what it tells us about who we all are. For the next number of months, we took turns taking a few weeks at a time to embed ourselves in Maggie's remarkable staff. We walked in the garbage piles of Cairo, dodged the crowds in Tahir Square, and dealt with government curfews, tanks in the streets, and traffic that borders on absolute insanity. We went with Mama Maggie to the remote places in the desert where she retreats to refuel. We interviewed dozens of the young people who have followed Mama Maggie to work in unspeakable circumstances. And, based on what their work taught us about the human condition, we knew that this story had to be told.

With Gratitude

I would like to thank Adel and Nadia Makary, as well as Mark Makary, Matt and Maria Jacoby, Maggie Morgan, Kirsten Powers, and Kelly Seiler for their encouragement and solidarity with this project from the idea stage up until the day we submitted the manuscript. Christian Pinkston and Sean McCabe have been, as always, great supporters as well. Ellen Vaughn has been a tremendous partner in this project. I'm thankful to have had her as a colleague in this endeavor—one that took me out of my comfort zone and taught me much about our world back home.

I am also grateful for Lord David Alton of the UK, Reverend Winrich Scheffbuch of Germany, the members of the entire Stephen's Children boards of reference around the world—all have been a creative springboard for this work that is helping poor kids all over. So many other generous and thoughtful people of faith around the world have helped Mama Maggie and her team in so many ways; it would be impossible to list them all. I know there have also been many spiritual fathers and mothers in Mama Maggie's life, such as Bishop Abraam of Fayoum and Giza, Pope Kyrolos VI, Father Antonius Amin, Rev. Menese Abdel Nour, His Grace Metropolitan Amba Michael of Assiut, and others. This book couldn't begin to cover all of their stories. We are grateful for them, as we've seen their impact on her journey, which in turn has of course helped the kids.

Mostly, I'm thankful to Mama Maggie—and all those who work with her—for showing me, and so many others, a way to live that is full of purpose, real meaning, and the unique joy that comes through serving others.

Marty Makary

I AM SO GRATEFUL THAT MARTY MAKARY INTRODUCED ME to Egypt and Mama Maggie and her colleagues. I am thankful for new friends in Cairo who work with Stephen's Children. I cannot say enough about their courage, ever-available sacrifice, love for their country, and love for people who have had the misfortune to be born in poverty. I was honored to try to put forward just a bit of the great story that Mama Maggie and her team are writing, one that will last forever.

I am thankful to Mama Maggie and her extraordinary husband, Ibrahim. Thank you also to Mama Maggie's extended family and friends, both in Egypt and the United States, who talked with me: Fifi, Nabil, Gamal, Moheb, Nadia, Adel, Mark, Maria, Matt, Joe, Bosh, Dina, Maggie Morgan, and so many others. Thank you for sharing your lives and stories with such great fun and grace! Thank you, Marty

Reimer, for your Egyptian hospitality. Thank you to Frank Wolf, Ron Blue, Terry Parker, Hugh Maclellan, Daryl Heald, Frances Heald, Father Anthony Messeh, Pastor Fakhri Yacoub, J. C. Huizenga, Kyle Parrish, the fathers and brothers of St. Anthony's and St. Paul's monasteries, the Cave Church, the Hanging Church, Dr. George, and others who so generously gave of your time to talk with me.

I really appreciate Marty Makary and our colleague, the noted camel-rider Christian Pinkston. It was a great pleasure to career around Cairo, the Sahara Desert, and Tahrir Square with these brothers. They are visionary and gifted men who are pouring their lives out for others, in so many ways. I am also very thankful for Kelly Seiler, who so cheerfully kept our traveling logistics sane.

As with any project I somehow complete, I'm so grateful for my family, who give me the bandwidth to write books. Thanks to Lee Vaughn, for his resilience as I repeatedly left the United States for Egypt and worked with deadlines with our distinguished and thoughtful friends at Thomas Nelson like Joel Miller, Webb Younce, Heather Skelton, and others. Thanks to Emily Vaughn Malloy, Cameron Malloy, Haley Vaughn, Walker Vaughn, Norma Vaughn, Patti Bryce, and so many friends who constantly give me grace and encouragement in my writing life.

Ellen Vaughn

Notes

Chapter 1: An Angel in the Dark

1. We have changed some people's names throughout this book.
2. This is transliterated in various ways from Arabic into English, just as is "*Zabaleen*" and other Arabic names and words.

Chapter 5: Garbage People?

1. Kent Annon, "Chaos and Grace in the Slums of the Earth," christianitytoday.com, August 29, 2013, http://www.christianitytoday .com/ct/2013/september/chaos-and-grace-in-slums-of-earth.html.
2. The endemic of predatory property grabbing receives little international attention, but it is a focus area of the global organization, International Justice Mission, http://www.ijm.org/casework/ property-grabbing.
3. Patrick Kingsley, "Waste Not: Egypt's Refuse Collectors Regain Role at Heart of Cairo Society," Guardian.com, March 27, 2014, http:// www.theguardian.com/global-development/poverty-matters/2014/ mar/27/waste-egypt-refuse-collectors-zabaleen-cairo.

Chapter 6: The Land Beyond Time

1. Samuel Tadros, *Motherland Lost: The Egyptian and Coptic Quest for Modernity* (Stanford, California: Hoover Institution Press, 2013), 11.
2. Matthew 2:1–15.
3. Isaiah 19:19 ESV.

Chapter 7: Promotion

1. Isaiah 61:1–4.

Chapter 9: I Can!

1. Al-Masry Al-Youm, "Egypt's Primary Education Ranks Last in Global Competitiveness Report," egyptindendent.com, August 9, 2013, http://www.egyptindependent.com/news/egypt-s-primary-education-ranks-last-global-competitiveness-report.
2. 2013 study by the Central Agency for Public Mobilisation and Statistics (CAPMAS), cited in http://www.albawaba.com/editorchoice/egypt-illiteracy-female-520546
3. "Egypt: Illiteracy Still Rife Among Rural Women," irinnews.com, March 8, 2006, http://www.irinnews.org/report/26179/egypt-illiteracy-still-rife-among-rural-women.
4. Philippians 4:13 NKJV.
5. Philippians 4:8 ESV.

Chapter 12: Metamorphosis

1. Dan Scott, "Mama Maggie," *Pastor Dan Scott* [blog], August 15, 2011, http://pastordanscott.blogspot.com/2011/08/mama-maggie.html.

Chapter 14: The Persistent Mr. Qiddees

1. Acts 18:9–10 NIV, emphasis added.
2. As with any story in Egypt, Mokattam's origins—and those of her unexpected church—go back more than a few years. The history of the mountain began to get interesting in AD 979. The story has many facets and much detail, but the very short version goes something like this:

In 979, Egypt's ruler was one Caliph Al-Muizz. A Muslim, he enjoyed religious debate, and gathered together Jews, Christians, and Muslims for discussions. At one point a Jew named Yaqub—who had converted in name to Islam in order to have a position in the sultan's cabinet—and the Coptic pope Abraam, were verbally jousting.

The Caliph looked on, amused. The Pope was doing well . . . and then Yaqub came in for the checkmate, so to speak. He quoted a verse from the New Testament: "If you have faith as small as a mustard seed, you can say to the mountain, 'Move from here to there,' and it will move. Nothing will be impossible for you."

Yaqub paused, triumphant. The Caliph must have lifted an eyebrow. This should be interesting. He asked the pope to move Mokattam Mountain. If he was unable to do so, it would be proof that Christianity was false, and the Christians would go to the sword.

The pope asked for three days in order to prepare. He and the Copts of Egypt fasted and prayed. He was moved to find a one-eyed Christian cobbler, a holy man named Simon the Tanner—or Simon the Shoemaker—to give him a hand.

On the third day—November 27, 979—Simon and the Christians gathered on one side of the mountain, the Caliph and his troops on the other, and we can assume that Yaqub was somewhere nearby, ready to gloat.

Simon and the Pope and the people began to shout out, "Lord, have mercy," repeating it three times.

Suddenly the mountain began to shake. It moved up and down. Observers down the hill said later that they could see the sun *beneath* the mountain. The Christians were saved from destruction. The Caliph decided to become one.

This story has been passed down for generations. It is a part of the Coptic identity. And one thousand years later, it fueled Farahat's own confidence in miracles in the garbage village.

Chapter 15: "The Dead Live Better than We Do"
1. Mark 2:1–12.

Chapter 17: Pigs and Politics
1. http://www.theguardian.com/global-development/poverty-matters/2014/mar/27/waste-egypt-refuse-collectors-zabaleen-cairo.

Chapter 20: God's Athletes

1. Bob Simon, "The Coptic Christians of Egypt," *60 Minutes*, December 15, 2013, http://www.cbsnews.com/videos/the-coptic-christians-of-egypt/; transcript available at http://www.cbsnews.com/news/the-coptic-christians-of-egypt/.

Chapter 22: Lives Touching Lives

1. International Justice Mission is a human rights agency that brings rescue to victims of slavery, sexual exploitation, and other forms of violent oppression. IJM lawyers, investigators, and aftercare professionals work with local officials to secure immediate victim rescue and aftercare, to prosecute perpetrators, and to ensure that public justice systems—police, courts, and laws—effectively protect the poor. http://www.ijm.org/.

Chapter 24: Mama Maggie in Action: *Stop!*

1. Matthew 5:3–10.

Chapter 26: Flames and Forgiveness

1. Sarah El Deeb, "Anti-Morsi Petition Gets 22 Million Signatures, Rebel Group Claims," huffingtonpost.com, June 29, 2013, http://www.huffingtonpost.com/2013/06/29/anti-morsi-petition_n_3521595.html.
2. Alaa Al Aswany, "Egypt's Two-Front War for Democracy," nytimes.com, November 10, 2013, http://www.nytimes.com/2013/11/11/opinion/aswani-egypts-two-front-war-for-democracy.html?_r=0.
3. Erica Ritz, "Will New 'Democratic' Egyptian Constitution Allow 9-Year-Old Girls to Marry?" theblaze.com, September 29, 2012, http://www.theblaze.com/stories/2012/09/29/will-new-democratic-egyptian-constitution-allow-9-year-old-girls-to-marry/.
4. Kirsten Powers, "The Muslim Brotherhood's War on Coptic Christians," thedailybeast.com, August 22, 2013, http://www.thedailybeast.com/articles/2013/08/22/the-muslim-brotherhood-s-war-on-coptic-christians.html.
5. "Morsi to Face Criminal and Not Political Charges," albawaba.com, November 3, 2013, http://www.albawaba.com/news/morsi-trial-egypt-criminal-charges-530739.

6. Todd Beamon, "Egyptian Girl, 10, Killed Heading Home from Bible Class," newsmax.com, August, 13, 2013, http://www.newsmax .com/Newsfront/egyptian-christian-girl-killed/2013/08/13/ id/520203#ixzz2yV99kbkF.

7. Sarah Sirgany and Laura Smith-Spark, "'Horrible': Christian Churches Across Egypt Stormed, Torched," cnn.com, August 15, 2013, http://www.cnn.com/2013/08/15/world/meast/egypt-church-attacks/index.html.

8. "Christians Come Under Attack in Egypt," catholicherald.co.uk, August 20, 2013, http://www.catholicherald.co.uk/news/2013/08/20/ christians-come-under-attack-in-egypt/.

9. Bob Simon, "The Coptic Christians of Egypt," *60 Minutes*, December 15, 2013, http://www.cbsnews.com/videos/the-coptic-christians-of-egypt/; transcript available at http://www.cbsnews.com/news/ the-coptic-christians-of-egypt/

10. http://egyptianstreets.com/2013/08/16/ coptic-churches-burn-amid-violence-in-egypt/.

11. Simon, "The Coptic Christians of Egypt."

Chapter 27: Simple Work, with Great Love

1. "Egypt: Coptic Christians Kidnapped Weekly, Held for Ransom by Radicals," persecution.org, January 1, 2014, http://www.persecution .org/2014/01/23/egypt-coptic-christians-kidnapped-weekly-held-for-ransom-by-radicals.

2. Kristen, Chick, "Egypt's Christians Close Ranks as Kidnappings Spike," Christiansciencemonitor.com, November 12, 2013, http://www.csmonitor.com/World/Middle-East/2013/1112/ Egypt-s-Christians-close-ranks-as-kidnappings-spike.

3. Ibid.

4. Larisa Epatko, "Coptic Christians Make an 'Easy Target' in Egypt's Unrest," Pbs.org, August 19, 2013, http://www.pbs.org/newshour/ rundown/coptic-christians/.